To Peter Lawrence

Fr Phil with love

13/02/2012

John 8:32 "And you shall know the truth, and the truth shall make you free."

British Families Under Labour

British Families Under Labour

Under Labour

And Lessons Learnt

PHILIP MATTIS

Library of Congress Control Number: 2011902033
ISBN: Hardcover   978-1-4568-6618-1
                    Softcover   978-1-4568-6617-4
                    Ebook   978-1-4568-4408-0

Bible quotations are from the New King James Version.

This book was printed in the United States of America.

To order additional copies of this book, contact:
Xlibris Corporation
0-800-644-6988
www.XlibrisPublishing.co.uk
Orders@XlibrisPublishing.co.uk
301621

Contents

Reasons for Writing This Book 1

1. Where there is happiness, there is harmony,
    and where there is harmony, there is happiness.......................3
2. Families Are the Fruits on Which to Flourish 6
3. The Family Is the Foundation of Stability...............................11
4. Spending to Be Happy 13
5. Save Yourself from a Sad Scenario...16
6. You Won't Learn until You Make Mistakes 20
7. Fruits from the Fundamentals...21
8. Comfort Comes with Constants 24
9. Home in on Harmony..32
10. Me, Myself, and I 38
11. Divorce 44
12. Today's Reality—So Scary It's 'Not' Real................................46
13. Fruits of Policy-maker New Labour...62
14. Men and Women 65
15. Change the Hard Way 76
16. Some More Answers 81
17. Living a Life of Lies 90
18. Working at Life 102
19. Twenty-first Century Reality 106
20. The Benefits of Avoiding Trivialities......................................112
21. Role Reversal 115
22. Children..118
23. Credit Crunch 124
24. The Weakest Link 126

25. Be Smart, Act Smart, and Not Like a Go-kart 128

26. Counselling.. 133

27. Marriages That Work and Lifestyles That Don't......................... 136

28. Looking Back at Lessons Learnt 145

29. Another Lesson... 148

30. Some Conclusions 149

31. Yet Another Lesson 152

32. Credit Crunch and Finances.. 154

33. Break Through the Clutter and Mediocrity 156

34. A poem for our times. Mankind or the Fallen Kind...................... 158

35. This Once Great Place 161

36. Messages from Our Lord.. 166

37. The Coming Day of the Lord... 173

Notes 179

Portrait Drawings 183

Reasons for Writing This Book

Shocked and bewildered by the depths of depravity and mediocrity which human beings have sunk to in their relations with each other despite the advancements made in technology and wealth, I was jolted to do what I could to make people aware of these pitfalls and give advice where necessary based on my experiences of twenty-six years of married life.

We, as a human race of people, are truly in an awful state, brought on primarily by selfishness, not taking responsibility for our actions but nearly always blaming others, and greed. So the disastrous state that we, as human beings, are in is primarily self-made.

But even worse, we all know what to do or what we should not do to right things, but we refuse to do it, mainly because of fear of losing pride, loss of face or material things. So our focus is a shortsighted one, as we fail to see the bigger picture down the road of the benefits of humility and long-term fulfilment of putting others first.

As I go about my daily life, one of the things I observe is that the people in the middle are the ones who are being squeezed by the havoc being wreaked by those at the very top and those at the very bottom.

For instance, when I drive on Britain's roads, the ones who adhere to the laws and rules of the road are usually the middle classes as they make their way to and from work in their ordinary cars. The rich, who drive mainly big expensive cars, often have no time or wish to follow these rules as they break speed limits with impunity or use bus lanes to get past queues of traffic. They are often ruthless in making or getting more wealth and power, and so treat people they come into contact with likewise.

Also, those at the very bottom, who sometimes have little or no driving documents or have been banned from driving, do likewise.

It tells me one thing for sure, and that is that the way we regard the rules of the road is also the way we regard others, and other rules and laws in our life, and treat them as such. So, for some it is, 'do as I say, but not as I do;' or one rule for one and another rule for others. For instance, the politicians who run our country give themselves into marriage, but in their policies they discourage marriage and encourage women to become single parents.

Unfortunately, this has, over the past decade or so, been more and more the way things are done in our country.

Where there is happiness, there is harmony, and where there is harmony, there is happiness

*I*n today's world most people are fooled into believing that happiness comes first from material things, hence a career, a job first, then family after. So more and more, children are left to fend for themselves, left with grandparents, with childminders, or even on their own, in front of the television, say.

A cooked meal is often no longer available, but fast food or hunger takes its place instead. This is what is called progress. However, children constantly left on their own or with someone else are not as happy and fulfilled as children in regular care of at least one of their parents.

Parenthood is no longer valued and looked on highly in today's world, but is instead looked down on, while a career is more valued and looked on more highly than marriage and parenthood. This is partly encouraged by 'progressive' politics and feminism.

So parents today treat parenthood as such—not looking after their children like they used to, but leaving this important duty instead to childminders, grandparents, and teachers. These people do have a role to play, but today, they play an increasingly greater role than before, and we are reaping the adverse effects from this trend in modern society. So clearly, this approach is wrong.

Children are growing up unhappier than ever before, as they interact less and less with their parents and so do not gain the necessary skills needed for later life. They get very little exercise also, but instead, they sit in front of a box to watch television or play video games for hours on end. So a lot of the skills they learn are those picked up from these sources. And you and I know that what's presented on the box in most cases is not good for children's consumption.

As a result, their communication skills are worse than those of their predecessors, and despite a greater priority being placed on education these days, many leave school, not being able to read and write properly. Children live what they learn and learn what they live, and increasingly they are learning the wrong things, which is proving very damaging to themselves and society as a whole, as parents put their careers first. This is the avenue promoted by the government, as they appear to value the traditional family less and less, and now we are starting to reap the whirlwind.

Some of the effects of this trend can be seen and heard being played out in the streets. Children are using knives, guns, and other implements on each other at an alarming rate. And many think that the source of all this anger stems from a broken home, parents not playing their part in their children's life as they used to, and what children see and play on the box coming to reality.

They also fight pitch battles with the police on a regular basis and some even attempt to make their communities no-go areas for the police and law-abiding citizens alike.

But the speech area is probably the most obvious aspect of modern society's effect on young people today. Have you ever heard some of today's young people speaking on television, say? It is a form of language that many of us do not recognise, let alone understand. These are kids brought up in modern Britain, and we are supposed to herald this new age of progress. What a travesty of the word!

So what do you expect? Many would rightly say, 'If you play with fire by tampering with well-founded principles, which have stood the test of time, you are sure to get burnt.' So strong families are the fruits on which children flourish.

Families Are the Fruits on Which to Flourish

Strong families are the fruits in which to flourish relationship-wise, physically, mentally, and spiritually. Without a strong family unit, one or more of all these three areas tend to fall apart. No matter how unhappy you may be at the moment with your family, if you think long and hard enough, you will come to the realisation that it is the best place for you.

Given the surveys over the past few decades, all of which point to the fact that children brought up in a family unit where there is a mother and a father present do far better than children in any other circumstance, so where do you think the best place for you is?

Not many surveys of single men have been done. In today's world they are simply vilified or forgotten. But from all reports available, they fare even worse than the family they leave once they separate from their partners. The alternatives may look attractive at first, but wide is the road to destruction and narrow is the gate that leads to life. 1. So stick to the narrow confines of the family.

You must struggle and fight to save your marriage at all cost, especially in this age whereby feminism has been running rampant tearing families apart. At the end of that process, you will be glad you did, and people who go through that process come out on the other side stronger and wiser from their experience. So if there is trouble within and trouble brewing, you need wisdom, patience and understanding to see things through, though these options may not seem worth it at first glance. But to gain wisdom, you must first of all fear God. The fear of the Lord is the beginning of wisdom. And knowledge of the Holy One is understanding. 2.

Wisdom is very necessary in rearing a family, but more and more wisdom goes out the window when there are family conflicts. Wisdom involves, first of all, not thinking about yourself in the event of a conflict. This is easy to say but difficult to do. You must put your family first. This may sometimes mean walking away from your cantankerous family temporarily, so that, at some stage, they will come to the realisation that the path they have chosen is the self-destructive path to the dungeon of the disgraced and fallen.

Do not, for instance, resist a cantankerous person. Choose the path of least resistance. More and more resistance leads only to more and more frictions, and hence more and more frustrations, as the other person refuses to yield. That is human nature. So there is no point going against human nature. In the middle of an heated argument all rationale goes out of the window, so you would simply be banging your head against a brick wall. This is something everyone knows, but we all, at some stage in our marriages, engage in mouth-to-mouth combat, and suffer a terrible bite-back from our partner's attack. At the end of that combat there is often a trail of pointless destruction, because we fail to heed instruction.

There is no point telling the other persons that they are wrong or it's their fault. In nearly all cases, do you think that they are going to say 'Yes, you are right'? The answer is certainly not. And I don't need to answer that question for you, either. You have dented their pride, especially if you have done it in front of the children or an adult. You have hurt their feelings, and they are going to hit back either verbally or physically. If one of you does not arrest the situation there and then, one thing will lead to another, which will then spiral out of control and devouring innocent souls.

When you are in a level-headed situation, you act rationally, thus leaving things as they were or making them better. However, when our anger is aroused, we often loose our cool, our rationale and ultimately, control. The result is that the situation we try to make better by our anger gets reversed into a downward spiral that you, from then on, struggle to bring back into equilibrium. And often it never comes back into that sought after equilibrium.

Families are divided and even separated. Then, a once-ideal-and-happy situation just gets from bad to worse, with no end in sight of this anger and blight to a family that fights. Anger does indeed kill off the fool, and all those around get adversely affected. A fool has no delight in understanding, but in expressing his own heart. 3.

If you can only control your anger, you can have life and have it more abundantly than you thought possible. Anger kills your spirit, kills hope, and kills your life. It festers and eats away at your very core. When anger erupts it alienates and creates stalemate. You become an object of rage, derision and a downward spiral into oblivion.

With control, you live to see another day, revitalised, rejuvenated, and even putting the past behind you and out of the way. You learn to keep away from people who make you unhappy. Yes, sometimes when there is no use talking sense into the head of the other person, it is often necessary to keep away from them for a while, until they cool down their temper like the weather often is in September. This does not mean walking out on them permanently; no, quite the opposite—it means walking away while sticking together to give the marriage space to breathe, to gather one's thoughts, to make amends, or not to indulge any further in order to make peace.

Then you can start learning how to learn about life and life's lessons instead of burning from your wife's nagging when she starts flagging.

If you're talented, you may have difficulty when it comes to staying teachable. Gifted people sometimes act as if they know it all. That makes it hard for them to keep developing. Teachability is not so much about competence and mental capacity, as it is about attitude; it's the hunger to discover and grow. It's the willingness to learn, unlearn and relearn.

John Wooden said, 'It's what you learn after you know it all that counts.' When you stop learning, you stop leading. Only as long as you remain teachable will you keep growing and continue to make an impact.

Besides being an astonishing painter and sculpture, Leonardo da Vinci was a genius in more fields than any scientist of any age. His notebooks were hundreds of years ahead of their time. He anticipated submarines, helicopters and other modern inventions. In one notebook he wrote, 'iron rusts from disuse; stagnant water loses its purity and in cold weather becomes frozen; even so does inaction sap the vigour of the mind.'

He was driven by his desire to know more. He was learning and writing discoveries in his notebooks until the very end of his life. And the good news is, you don't have to have the mind or talent of Leonardo da Vinci to be teachable. You just have to have the right attitude.

The most important skill to acquire is learning how to learn. Try this for the next week; ask others for their advice and deliberately withhold the advice you'd normally give. At each day's end write down what you've learned by being attentive to others. You'll be amazed. (**Source: UCB's The Word for Today**).

In a marriage, you are never going to agree on everything. In fact, as the marriage gets older there are going to be many things that you disagree on. Also, one gets set in one's ways even more. So there is no point trying to force one's opinion on the other. So learn to agree to disagree sometimes. If your way is right, it will prove itself in due course, and you will have saved yourself a broken marriage and a broken home by observing, listening more and remaining teachable. Nothing is done before its time; so do not force the issue and things will be fine.

If your marriage is foundering, no amount of arguing is going to make things better. Notice a fire and how it burns: if you add fuel to it, it burns even stronger. Left well alone, it burns itself out. One has to apply a strategy of patience in the face of affliction and persecution, while not making the situation any worse, as the alternatives, while they seem attractive in the heat of the moment, are fruitless and self-destructive.

Be kindly affectionate to one another with brotherly love, in honour, giving preference to one another; not lagging in diligence, fervent in spirit, serving the Lord; rejoicing in hope, *patient in tribulation*, continuing steadfastly in prayer. 4. Bless those who persecute you; bless and do not curse. 5. Repay no one evil for evil . . . If it is possible, as much as depends on you, live peaceable with all men. 6. Do not *be overcome by evil*, but overcome evil with good. 7.

These are the best strategies to apply. But sometimes as there is no talking sense in the other person, or you can see clearly that they are only interested in destroying you, in which case you must rebuke the wicked one. No weapon formed against you shall prosper, and every tongue which rises against you in judgement you shall condemn . . . 8 . . . . If your brother sins against you, rebuke him; and if he repents forgive him. 9.

The Family Is the Foundation of Stability

I am sure that you know people who are separated, and I am also sure that they are not faring very well. They are often beset by illness, crime, violence, self-destructive behaviour generally, and even death. So why would you want to go there too?

'Oh, it won't be like that for me.' Well, surprise, surprise! If you think you lost control of your life when you were in a family unit, wait until you leave that unit. You are far more likely to lose control of your life even more once separated than when you were in that family unit. Unless, of course, you are guided by the Lord: Assuredly, I say to you, there is no one that has left house or brothers or sisters or father or mother or wife or children or lands for My sake and the gospel's who shall not receive a hundredfold now in this time—houses and brothers and sisters and mothers and children and lands, with persecutions—and in the age to come, eternal life. But many who are first will be last, and last first. 10.

If you think you had problems then, wait until you are gone. You will be truly gone and so will your family. If you were not able to control things when you were with your family, what background do you therefore possess to control your life while single or with a new partner? United we stand, but divided we fall, and fall you will fall from the frying pan straight into the fire, unless you have Christ. Because If you do not have Christ, you are being guided by destructive forces: Jesus said to him, "I am the way, the truth, and the life. No one comes to the Father except through Me." 130.

Politicians when they make policies for the family, or as it nearly always turn out, these policies work against the family, they never mention this country's strong Christian tradition in rearing families as part of their policy. Then when they end up with failure and disaster in our homes and on our streets, they wonder why.

Spending to Be Happy

When relationships are washed up, some people go on a spending spree to be happy and get away from their problems. But spending only adds more problems to your already heavily laden shoulders, while the happiness you crave for still eludes you in the long term.

If, for example, you go out and buy a second car, when one will do, it means more time will be taken up with things you would rather not be doing, such as carrying out repairs to your cars and trying to manage money involved in their upkeep—perhaps money you have not got in the first place—thus plunging you further in debt. Also, it could be money you were hoping to spend on your children, but now you have not got it any more. You have got to spend time to clean both, which is perhaps the time you would rather spend with your children.

This then leads to increased frustrations on your part, as you are not able to spend time in ways you were hoping to. In addition, you no longer have the money to spend in ways that would have been more profitable to you and your family, rather than yourself only.

When your children have not got the time and things you were hoping to share with them, this only brings frustration to yourself, your children, and your spouse. This then leads to bickering and acrimony between your family and yourself. Bickering, which could have been avoided had you chosen to spend the money on your family, or saved it for a rainy day rather than spending it on yourself or with yourself in mind, in the first place.

I think it's called treating yourself. Treating yourself comes with an initial euphoria, but it is usually followed by serious lows, when what you buy does not live up to your expectations in pleasure, but comes, instead, with a lot of financial and work baggage.

He who finds his life will lose it, and he who loses his life for My sake will find it. 120.

Whereas treating your family is far more likely to bring long-term satisfaction and benefits for your family and yourself. They will remember what you have done for a very long time in just the same way that they will remember for a long time when you have done something bad, in your interest only or completely against them, such as infidelity.

Look at Joseph. When Potiphar's wife tried to seduce him he did not a) try to counsel or convert her b) think, 'I'm young, lonely, far from home, and her husband's out of town; maybe just this once' c) hang around to see how strong he was. No, he fled the scene saying, 'How ... could I do such a wicked thing ... against God?' 121.

It's good to stretch yourself. It's how you mature. But be aware of danger zones and don't knowingly put yourself in harm's way. Paul said, 'If you think you are strong ... be careful not to fall.' 122. He told Timothy, 'Run from temptation that capture young people ... do the right thing.' And James said, 'Don't let anyone under pressure to give in to evil say, "God is trying to trip me up." God ... puts evil in no one's way. The temptation comes from us and only us' 123.

The bottom line is this: when you're weak in certain areas you need to steer clear of anything that feeds into them. The Psalmist said, 'You are my safe refuge ... where my enemies cannot reach me.' 122. 122. (Psalm 61:3NLT). So, what do you need to avoid? (**Source: UCB's The Word for Today**).

That very thing you bought, which is causing so much trouble for you and your family, could one day be bought for you by members of that same family or friends on your birthday, say, because they know that that is something you were longing for, but instead, you decided to put them first. Think of the happiness and joy that that would bring, instead of the frustrations you now have. This is also a lesson in patience and in reaping what you have sown.

Treating others wins and keeps friendships for a very long time. That is what the supermarkets and department stores do when they want to capture and keep your custom. They have learnt this lesson probably better than anyone else. Let nothing be done through selfish ambition or conceit, but in lowliness of mind let each esteem others better than himself. 11.

Save Yourself from a Sad Scenario

*I*t is very common for couples to ignore common values, ideals, and probably most importantly, common background and upbringing when forming relationships, as they are first and foremost swept away by sexual pleasures and sexual compatibility. This then becomes the main basis for forming relationships, which is entirely the wrong way to go about a potentially lifelong commitment.

If, for instance, you both come from a background whereby you were brought up in marriage, your relationship stands a much better chance of succeeding than if one of you were from a marriage background and the other one from a broken home, or both of you from broken homes.

If, for instance, one was from a marriage background and the other one from a broken home, once the dust has settled, the honeymoon is over, and the arguments start, at some stage, one will very likely start to espouse the virtues of being single or being a single parent over being married.

Some years down the line, one may even say to the other, 'Why don't we just go our separate ways? We will still stay friends, and you can see the children when you want,' if it is that amicable. These sound bites usually come from the party who was brought up in a broken home.

In relationships where one party was brought up without one parent, usually the father, the husband becomes vilified for not being the husband

and the father he is expected to be. He is expected to fill the role of the father she did not have, as well as being a good husband.

In such relationships, men are not thought well of, as the mother was the hero in the girl's life, and who was always there when the father abdicated his responsibilities. Now the new man in her life has to bear the brunt of her disillusionment with men in general and her father in particular. This can be a daily onslaught, which wears her man to the bones, until he snaps or until he leaves. This scenario became very rampant under New Labour. But, men, don't go unless you are shown the door. Keep persevering.

On June 1, 1965, a 13-foot boat slipped quietly out of Falmouth, Massachusetts. It destination? Falmouth, England. It would be the smallest craft ever to make the voyage. Its name? Tinkerbelle. Its pilot? Robert Manry, a copy editor for the Cleveland Plain Dealer newspaper who felt that 10 years at a desk was enough boredom for anyone. Manry was afraid, not of the ocean, but of all the people who would try to talk him out of the trip. So he only shared it with some relatives and his wife Virginia, his greatest source of support.

The trip? He spent harrowing nights of sleeplessness trying to cross shipping lanes without getting run over. Weeks at sea caused his food to become tasteless. Loneliness led to hallucinations. His rudder broke three times. Storms swept him overboard. Had it not been for the rope around his waist, he would never have been able to pull himself back on board.

Finally, after 78 days alone at sea he sailed into Falmouth, England. During those nights at the tiller he had fantasised about what he would do once he arrived. He expected to simply check into a hotel, eat dinner alone, then next morning see if perhaps the Associated Press might be interested in his story. **What a surprise!** Word had spread far and wide. To his amazement, 300 vessels with horns blasting escorted Tinkerbelle into port and 47,000 people stood screaming and cheering him to the shore.

One of the great themes of Scripture is perseverance. No matter how great your calling, your talent, your cause or your goal, **without perseverance you won't make it.** Hence James writes, 'Blessed is the man who perseveres.' 124. **(Source: UCB's The Word for Today).**

No doubt Manry learnt many lessons of life from his arduous journey. But one of them was not, 'return early for fear of certainty of his life ending in the finality of the oceans gravity.' But instead plough ahead and put behind that dread and look to the joy and crown ahead, of finishing the course stated to overcome all that's complicated.

So remember life is a challenge to overcome the ravage placed on us by the savage, which sometimes is our marriage.

Put succinctly, a man's wife sometimes does not know how to show love to her husband, as she was not shown love herself by her father when she was growing up.

These kinds of women often prefer to be head of the family as their mother was the head of the family when they was growing up. This can be another breeding ground for more friction. And in the modern age that we are living in, they have the tacit support of the government in more ways than one. Support such as the tax and benefit system, which is designed to benefit single parents over couples, let alone married couples. I can't think of a more stupid system that the government has designed, and the results are coming through thick and fast to prove this.

How can all kinds of families be of equal value to society when broken homes are costing so much in health, well-being, and wealth? Another cost factor from broken homes is the number of children some women have. Many of them breed like rabbits, thus costing every taxpayer billions more in benefits.

Whoever designed a system that encourages such behaviour does not deserve to be in charge of all of our well-being and need their heads examined.

So make sure you both have as much in common before getting married, or what separates you before marriage will probably separate you both during marriage.

You Won't Learn until
You Make Mistakes

Nothing is achieved by playing safe. When you sink, there is no 'plan B' to make a comeback, as you have never learnt any lessons in life. And it's not the mistakes you make that count. It is how you get out of them. Fortune favours the brave. Benjamin Franklin said that those who give up liberty for safety deserve neither liberty nor safety. And that is what the benefit system, for instance, has become for an increasing number of people under New Labour—a safety trap rather than a safety net.

So people must be allowed to make their own mistakes so that they can learn from them. Life is a learning process, and it is hoped that you will come out on the other side in better shape, having learnt from your experiences. So, once bitten, twice shy. If you have never been bitten before, how will you know to be shy?

Fruits from the Fundamentals

*I*n the past, people sought and generally found true happiness and fulfilment from the fundamental values of life such as marriage, abstinence, thrift, love and forgiveness. Today, especially under New Labour, people seek happiness and fulfilment from the pleasures of life such as promiscuity, infidelity, binge-drinking, smoking, partying, fist fights, drunken behaviour, speeding, spending and not so pleasurable things such as abortion and divorce, and many other avenues that present themselves as easy and good fun. To accompany that, people, in droves, are abandoning the fundamental values that society was built on.

Why abandon security, stability, and satisfaction for pleasures, getting a high, and the associated risk to life and limb? One does not know, but that is the human psyche this day and age.

One must say that it seems partly encouraged by the government, which does not appear to value families in terms of a married structure as in the past.

But these are only easy avenues to destruction. And this destruction is set to continue unabated as the government buries its head in the sand in the face of evidence upon evidence that points to the fact that society is better off and costs less when built on the fundamental values of marriage.

They will lift their heads out of the sand at some point, but I think that by the time they do that, it will be too late. Britain will be too far gone in the pits of immorality for any meaningful recovery to take place. They have presided over Britain being a society of broken homes, bankers and benefit scroungers. While stable families help to stave off disaster by the sacrifices they make with stable homes, in the workplace and with their tax take.

They will admit their mistakes eventually, but no one likes to admit that they have got things wrong, especially while in government. Unfortunately, the pride comes before the fall. They will need to fall significantly first before we can get an admission of faults and get changes in policy for a renewal of the party.

In the meantime, society, as a whole, has got to suffer and pick up the pieces from problems caused by a government that is aloof from the predicaments of the common man.

For the life of me, how can you pay people more to be apart than to be together? Since when does a long-standing rule of life become 'divided we stand but united we fall'? But this is exactly what the Labour government rules on benefits imply, as single mothers see their benefits nearly double during their tenure. To get this windfall they are required to do little or no work, except kick their man to the kerb. And we can see the effect of it everywhere in our society today.

Adults are encouraged to live apart, and when the devastating consequences of this policy filter down to the children and society at large, the government takes it out on the parents by introducing draconian measures on them to control their children and be better parents: talk about a government not fit for the purpose.

Now that there is a recession, these problems in families, where there is only one parent or where the parents are cohabiting, will only get worse. The government doesn't realise the Pandora's box it has opened with this stupid policy, which implies that united we fall, but divided we stand.

Those who cohabit-ate will find it easier to drift apart, as the tensions caused by the recession hit families. On the other hand if they are married they are more likely to stick together during difficult times. That is what marriage is all about: sticking together during good times as well as during bad times.

Cohabiting means to at least one partner that, 'I am not firmly attached here, and I don't want to be firmly attached either, because if there are any problems, I'm off.' That's not character building, that's character sinking.

Before David became qualified to rule as King in Zion, he first had to be found faithful in three places. Examine them carefully, for you too must pass these three tests:

1. *At home in Bethlehem.* That's where David learned to be responsible, to earn a living and support his family, to develop his relationship with God, and to overcome the resentment of others because of God's favour on his life. 'Charity begins at home.' It's here you become qualified to handle bigger assignments by being faithful in smaller ones. It's here you character is developed and your dependability proven.

2. *In the cave of Adullam.* By living among the misfits and rejects of society David learned to give of himself to others without expecting anything in return; to love and serve others even when his own life was under attack. 'Adullam' is where our kingdom dies and God's kingdom is showcased through us. It's here that God deals with every self-seeking, self-serving motive in our hearts. Sadly, some of us never make it out of this cave.

3. *On Mount Hebron.* The word Hebron means 'covenant'. It was the highest mountain in Israel and there was no easy road to the top; it was uphill all the way. And it's that way with covenant relationships! They require loyalty regardless of circumstance, truthfulness regardless of cost, and forgiveness regardless of pain. When we begin to live this way the world will look again to Zion (the church) for answers, because they'll see God working in us. (**Source: UCB's The Word for Today**).

Comfort Comes with Constants

*C*omforts come with constants. What I mean by that is that life is more settled and comfortable, hence happier, when one or more constants are in place. And the more constants there are in place, the more secure and, as a result, happier your life will be. The absence of these constants will lead to a chaotic and, as a result, a disastrous life.

These constants that I am referring to are marriage, whether stable or not; a job, preferably a secure one; a stable address and belief in Christ.

One of the most important ones is marriage. People who are married, especially men, are happier, more committed to their family, and live longer, healthier, and lead more fulfilled lives than people who cohabit-ate or are single. And this is despite the fact that their marriage may be turbulent or generally unstable.

Couples become more responsible and, as a result, are less likely to indulge in binge drinking, drugs, promiscuity, chain-smoking, abortion, separation, speeding, and reckless driving and all the various things that contribute to the breakdowns we see in society.

The secret is that in marriage, couples find happiness in all its forms naturally. Yet people run away from marriage in favour of shacking up or a single life, because marriage is too binding—keeping them tied to one person for life. This is selfish thinking, because that person would rather opt in and out of a relationship when it suits them. But research shows that people who opt for this lifestyle are more unhappy and frustrated than people in marriage.

Outside marriage, people don't necessarily find happiness naturally, so they go looking for it in all the ways mentioned above, only to find that ultimately, they end up with disaster or, at the very least, dissatisfaction on their hands.

In marriage, disaster often comes when one or both partners decide to break their marriage vows and opt for divorce. That is the point at which all the unwanted aspects of life that they were trying to avoid, such as ill health, nervous breakdowns, drink and drug problems, promiscuity and STDs, loss of one's job, and children going astray and getting in trouble with the law, usually set in.

If they had stayed together in marriage and tried to work out their problems, things would not have ballooned out of control. For some people, their life may not yet have ballooned out of control, but there could be a significant fall in their life expectancy, especially for men.

Initially, after separating, one may be ecstatic that he or she is finally rid of the monster they got married to. But usually, that ecstasy falls as sharply as it rose when the new realities of life set in. And those new realities often compound the problems you thought you left behind.

One of those new realities are the facts of life when one gets hooked up to a new partner. When the dust has settled and the honeymoon is over, the unresolved emotional and financial baggage you both bring to the new relationship start to rear their ugly heads. So you now have double trouble on your head and shoulders

The second trouble is that your leaving of the marital home does not just affect you. Your decision is more far-reaching than you may imagine. It affects your wife or husband and children, then other relatives, and friends you once had; and it will come back to haunt you in ways you least expected.

For instance, why should children continue to be stable in a suddenly unstable situation, when all their life they have known stability? It does not work like that. Children are humans, too, and just as you were affected by an unhappy marriage, they will be affected adversely by suddenly not having you there any more. Also affected adversely will be the single parent that starts to struggle with everyday tasks.

You may think that you will not be affected on the day you walk away from your family, but you too are human and were not built to live on your own or away from your family. So you too will be affected before long, and the sudden euphoria you may have felt at the beginning to be rid of the situation, will one day come crashing down on you, when you realise what you have lost and the resulting emptiness and void in your life. This is unless you truly had no choice but to walk away from a relationship broken down by sexual immorality ... whoever divorces his wife for any reason except sexual immorality causes her to commit adultery. 12.

This emptiness often leads you to unusual ways of filling the void. These are things you would not have considered in the past, but they suddenly become acceptable. In the past when you were together in marriage, you knew instinctively that these things were not the right ways forward, because they would lead to difficulties in your marriage and would be bad for you and your family. So why would they suddenly be good for you? The truth is that it would be far worse for you now than before, because whereas in marriage it would partially ruin you and you could recover, as long as you are honest with your partner and work things out; but outside of marriage, there is little or no supporting background, so it could ruin you completely without you even realising it. So think thee, what will your legacy be?

In 1927, a Georgia real estate and insurance company folded, short-changing 500 stockholders. The owner, a man called Mercer, was a person of integrity who vowed if possible to repay every single penny. But despite his best efforts, his company never did make a comeback. After he died, his son remembered his father's vow and twenty-eight years later deposited a cheque in a Savannah bank to reimburse every last stockholder.

The young man was the successful singer/ songwriter, Johnny Mercer. One of the songs he wrote from which he earned the royalties to pay the stockholders was, 'Accentuate the Positive.' You've probably heard it.

When you go, leave your children something more than money to remember you by; leave them a legacy of integrity! Listen: **'The just man walketh in his integrity: his children are blessed after him.' (Source: UCB's The Word for Today).**

If you can't be trusted on all counts, you can't truly be trusted on any. Ethical principles are not flexible. A little white lie is still a lie; theft is theft, whether it's one pound or one million. Philips Brookes said, 'Character is made in the small moments of our lives,' like the moments outlined in this next story:

A teenager who'd just obtained his driver's licence told his parents he was meeting his friends at a **local restaurant.** But this particular restaurant had several locations **and he drove to one 60 miles away.** They say, **'What you don't expose will expose you.'** Unfortunately, his parents went shopping in that area the same evening. **Imagine his thoughts when he stopped at a junction, looked over, and saw his mum giving him that 'look' parents reserve for the worst offences!** We need to '. . . keep everything we do and say out in the open, the whole truth on display . . .; 131; speak the plain, unembellished truth, so people don't have to '. . . read between the lines or look for hidden meanings . . .' 132.

Sociologists suggest that people of poor character might have been different if they'd grown up in a better environment.

Character is a choice. Your circumstances are no more responsible for your character than the mirror for your looks. What you see only reflects what you are and what you are is what you've spent your life building! (**Source: UCB's The Word for Today**).

In marriage you would tend to stop what you are doing that is wrong and detrimental to your relationship. Because whatever you are doing that is wrong, but sweet, there is something sweeter, and that is your marriage and your children. But outside of marriage, nothing seems sweeter than what you are doing. So one step leads to another, and before long, you are on a slippery slope that makes it difficult to halt. And before you know it, you and possibly some of your children need rescuing from the situation you both find yourselves in.

But once deep into the addiction you find yourselves in, it is difficult to get out of it. It is easy to get in, but it is difficult to get out of addiction. So, many of us opt for this 'easy' option, instead of working on our relationships for the good of all concerned. But, if one were to shine a light in these now very dark, hidden areas of your life, you would scamper for cover, like insects in the dark when the light is shone on them.

We opt for the 'easy' option because we think of ourselves only. If we humble ourselves by thinking less about our selves and more about the ones who might be affected by our decisions, we would all lead happier and more fulfilled lives in the end. Because the result of taking a selfless action will be so beneficial to your family and society at large when you see the results, that you will never again want to go backwards into yourself. So humble yourself, before you are humiliated and start climbing out of your compromised, confused and corrupted state you find yourself in. Humility doesn't mean thinking less of yourself, it just means thinking of yourself less. So don't look inwardly. Look forward and outwardly in order to live responsibly.

Responsibility is a two-sided coin. On one side is responsibility, on the other side is rewards. Too many of us are focused on one side of the coin only—rewards: getting high and letting it all fly; no control because I am not responsible to a single sole. Taking responsibility means three things:

1. Acknowledging what you are responsible for.
2. Acknowledging who you are responsible to.
3. Acting responsibly at all times.

All the excuses you give yourself, and others, won't let you off the hook. Jesus said, 'Much is required from those to whom much is given.'

At their annual conference the manager of a dog food company asked his sales team how they liked the company's new advertising programme. 'Great!' they replied, 'the best in the business.' 'What do you think of the product?' he asked. 'Fantastic' they replied. 'How about the sales force?' he asked. They were the sales force, so of course they responded positively saying they were the best. 'Okay then,' the manager said, 'so if we have the best brand, the best packaging, the best advertising programme and the best sales force, why are we in seventeenth place in our industry?' After an awkward silence one of the salesmen shouted, 'It's those dogs; they just won't eat the stuff!'

Guess what? Your problem is not the dogs, or your job, or your spouse, or society at large, or whatever. Be honest, your biggest challenge in life is you. If your life is not going the way you want it to, you are responsible for changing it. God will help you if you turn to Him. But you must want to change, decide to change, and work each day toward that end. (**Source: UCB's The Word for Today**).

No one is an island, and happiness does not come from taking selfish actions. But when selfish actions lead to disaster only you can take responsibility. For no one will join you then for certainty. They will take you to the way of ruin and happily join in to see you end up in the painful bin of sin. But as for taking responsibility, it's a pity, but you will have to bear it all alone, as none of them are willing to stand or be found. Then you will be an island all on your own, which is a lonely cold existence over the life you have now blown. The initial euphoria from such actions will be quickly replaced by deep lows, when the full ramifications of what we have done sets in. We all like quick fixes, but quick fixes do not work. They lead to long-lasting sufferings for many. There is a popular saying which goes like this, 'You don't know what you have got till it's gone.'

Being honest, saying sorry for what you have done, and learning and practicing forgiveness are the keys to working out your problems and long-lasting happiness. The fixes will not be quick, but you will not reach the lows that accompany quick fixes.

As you start to pull out of your problems, which will be slow, a weight will be lifted from your shoulders and a heavy burden will be lifted from your heart (which we are not built to carry around), as forgiveness sets in. Carrying heavy burdens in our hearts is not good for our health, and that is exactly what many of us do when we walk away from relationships. This puts a price on the quality of our lives, our health, and the quantity of our lives or our life expectancy.

Thinking about others and living our lives for others bring a form of happiness that is unparalleled and which, unfortunately, eludes many of us. That is because we harbour selfish ways, which we refuse to break, deluding ourselves that that is the best way to be and the best way to high self esteem. Anything that does not put others first, especially our family, will not lead to lasting happiness. The happiness you appear to find will be short lived and unfulfilling. By nearly always putting yourself first, you will experience more bouts of unhappiness and sadness than you had bargained for; because you put rewards before responsibility, instead of putting them together.

So, if you have wronged your spouse or if you have been wronged, make up quickly and come clean, rather than do the 'easy' thing, which is to hold a grudge and/or walk away. This is the only way to long-term peace and happiness. Grudges eat away at your very core, as it gorges on your inside, and so keep you in constant anger and bitterness towards your partner or ex-partner.

If you have a history of being good to your family and have often shown forgiveness when things went wrong, instead of losing your rag at every opportunity, when things go against you, you are more likely to be shown forgiveness yourself. It is very difficult to break a very loving family, whatever is thrown at them. If we bear in mind that no one is perfect and we all make mistakes, in addition to a loving atmosphere, when the shock comes, we will be more disposed to forgive and show mercy. It is far easier to say than to do, but do we must for the cohesion of society and long-term peace and happiness.

Over two thousand years ago, Christ suffered far more at the hands of his own people than any man has ever done, yet he was able to forgive. Let all bitterness, wrath, anger, clamour, and evil speaking be put away from you, with all malice. And be kind to one another, tender hearted, forgiving one another, even as God in Christ forgave you. 13.

The people whom we will suffer most from will nearly always be members of our own family . . . a man's enemies will those of his own household.' In particular, children will be set against their parents and against each other, and in-laws will be set against in-laws. 135.

At work, we treat members of the public and our colleagues better than we treat our own families. We think twice before treating them badly, because we know that we will lose our jobs if we do. But we don't think twice about treating our families badly, because we know we can push things to the limit before being thrown out, which we can't do with our customers and colleagues at work. So before we treat our family badly, think of how we treat others at work firstly, and why we do what we do at work versus what we do with our families.

If we have a stable family life, the chances are greater for stable work-life, too, and vice versa.

Home in on Harmony

Quarrelling over minor issues, otherwise known as trivialities, is one of the major causes of strife and separation in the family home. I cannot speak from a woman's point of view because I am a bloke. The phrase 'she who must be obeyed' has now become a rule of thumb for men to follow. This is to ensure a peaceful, if not a very happy life. Many of our male folks have decided to relinquish their headship of the home and submit to the rule of their wives, who, with the support of the feminist movement, have bulldozed their way to the top of the home in no uncertain terms and taking no prisoners with them. And with female partners and single mothers having the full support of the authorities over their male partners, men find themselves unequally yoked and so are dumbfounded and confounded as to what their role in the home is, if they do have one anymore, given the forces stacked against them.

As a man, you cannot win an argument with a woman. You were not built or made to do so. So stop doing it for a peaceful life. Learn to walk away from arguments and learn to take the verbal missiles being thrown at you by your wife. It will certainly hurt, but it will hurt a lot more, and probably unbearably so, if you engage in a mouth-to-mouth combat. She is always going to emerge the victor, and in the society that we live in, if she calls the police, you are far more likely to be arrested than she is.

She only has to tell one lie about you for you to be arrested. While, if you make something up about her or tell the truth even, you are not likely to be taken seriously. In the heat of the moment, couples do make up things about each other to score cheap points. The truth often becomes a casualty to the whims and fancies of an heated argument.

Also it is very likely that you could be put out of the family home to fend for yourself. This is a far worse scenario than to be merely arrested, as she may sometime forgive you and have you back. But men who are put out to fend for themselves often do not fare very well, as all the surveys will show you. Many of them end up gravely ill and some even end up dead. Your life expectancy often reduces significantly once you leave the family home.

The onus is always put on the man to prove his innocence in family feuds. The woman has to prove nothing. Her word is taken as gospel by the authorities and that is the wrong approach. But that is the feminist society we live in today.

As a result of the society we have ended up with, counselors reckon that less than 25 per cent of marriages today are truly happy. Contentment is the key to a happy marriage. When asked what makes us contented in marriage, we inevitably point to things our partner does, or their characteristics, that pleases us. When asked what makes us discontented, we indicate what they do, or are, that displeases us. We focus on what's right or wrong about them, making ourselves happy or unhappy.

But contentment is an inside job! It's how we react to others. Our attitude is the real issue. The problem is not what we see or hear, it's how we see or hear it.'. . . The eye is not satisfied with seeing, nor the ear . . . with hearing' 136. The eye and ear—our perceptions—are the culprits. That's why God says,'. . . be content with such things as ye have . . .'137. We must choose to see things differently, in ways that don't make us unhappy. The controls are in our hands, not our partner's!

Contentment is a choice.'. . . I have learned in whatever state I am, to be content.' 138. We learn contentment by considering how much harder others have it, asking God how he wants us to use our challenges, and lacks of our growth and our partner's growth, and—remembering Erma Bombeck's advice—'The grass usually looks greener over someone else's septic system'. Benjamin Franklin said of marriage, 'keep your eyes wide open beforehand, and half shut afterwards'.

Finally, we can learn contentment by praying for the courage to change what we can (especially our own attitude), the grace to accept what we cannot (most things are acceptable when we stop resenting them), and the wisdom to know the difference. (**Source: UCB's The Word for Today**).

So which is better: put up and shut up or engage and dig your own grave? To illustrate the society we are living in today, the following is a text sent to me on my mobile phone by my wife, 'Husband just finished reading book "Man of the House", when he stormed into kitchen, pointed a finger into his wife's face, and said, "From now on I want you to know that I am the man of the house, my word is law! You *will* prepare a gourmet meal for me tonight and every night! After, you will run me a bath. After the bath you will lie on the bed and take what's coming to you. And then in the morning guess who is going to wash and dress me?" She replied, "The f—ing undertaker."'

This illustrates the fact that men have largely lost their pre-eminent position in the home in this country. Women know this and have latched on to their rise in the home to headship in no uncertain terms. And if anyone tries to get in their way or tries to take their gains from them, they know what they can expect.

So once again learn contentment by praying for courage to change what we can, the grace to accept what we cannot, and wisdom to know the difference.

In getting to where they have gotten today, women have become very aggressive, and they are often rude and devious. Women are prepared to use many underhand tactics to remove their man from the headship of the home. Women condemn these normally male attributes when they see it in their husbands or partners, yet without a thought, take on these qualities themselves.

Men are no match for today's women in the home. In addition, the system we function in has been re-balanced in favour of women. So today's men are bewildered and confused about what has overtaken their women and what their role in the home has become. They are so bewildered and numbed that their silence on these issues is deafening.

Most men have adopted a defeated position, when it comes to getting on and dealing appropriately with their female companions. Their first option in many cases is to walk away from the relationship, leaving the children, in particular, to pick up the pieces of a broken home.

They haven't fathomed what has happened to them, so instead of trying to understand this modern phenomenon, they isolate themselves from it, leading to devastating consequences for themselves and their families.

Sometimes isolating yourself is a good thing, as long as it is a temporary measure to think and gather your thoughts. Every now and again, people from both sexes need time to themselves to try to make sense of what has been happening around them and to them. In short, they need time to reflect and recover. This often helps to recharge your batteries after you have been put down so often and made to feel worthless.

This helps you to cool off and put those negative thoughts and feelings that built up during the heat of the moment, to rest. Positive thoughts can then start to come through and build one after the other. Allow time to heal. You will start to work on ways of dealing with your situation, and you will realise too that you are better off together than without each other. Because, in those quiet moments, you will look into the abyss and think, it is not worth it, then take several steps back to sanity.

It is amazing how refreshing those quiet moments can be, which are entirely different from permanent quiet moments on your own, after you have decided to walk away from the family.

Then, those quiet moments become a hellhole of depression, sadness, bitterness, recrimination, and a whole sense of loss and defeat. The bond with your family has been broken, and as things stand, you have become the weakest link in the chain. Your thoughts and health will reflect that too, over time. So instead of strong, positive thoughts, you will develop weak negative thoughts that eat away at your very core. In addition, your health will follow suit, taking a nosedive into depression and other physical ailments associated with your mental state, your newly found circumstances, and lack of physical care. This means an unhappier life and a new search for happiness in the wrong things and places, which often leads to more disasters and a shortened life expectancy.

Ask any man who is divorced, separated or remarried if he is happy or happier, and the answer will almost universally be 'no'. And the statistics to match prove it. Over 50% of first time marriages end in divorce, 65% of second ones, and more than 70% of third ones. With a few exceptions, the more we do marriages the worse we get at it. As I have been indicating all along, you have a better chance of finding happiness in your first marriage. God's way is always the best way . . . what God has joined together, let not man separate, . . . 14.

Because where as with first marriages you look for the best and life-long happiness from the outset, with second and third marriages, you start looking at life from a loser's outlook, given that your first and possibly your second marriages were lacklustre failures. And so these second and third adventures you were not very hopeful but became a hope-fool, being so overladen with baggages from your past that your new ship was certain to flip and sink.

But submitting to your wife does not necessarily mean a worse life for men. Firstly, it means a more peaceful life that confrontation does not bring, and it can eventually lead to some sort of a life once you get used to your new role in the home. Submitting to your wife is part of the way forward in this modern world. But be careful how much of modern society you pick up, as most of it is not good. Man has decided to forsake what is good and understood for what is unknown, which eventually brings him down with a frown.

The Bible advises against resisting others. And there are good reasons for this, as it only brings more confrontation to what is often an already bad situation. Think of some of the innumerable heartaches and headaches you will have saved yourself from by submitting to your wife and having a life. If your way is right, don't fight. She will eventually be brought to her knees or senses when all she has been craving for comes crashing to the floor. And the word of God which says wife submit to your husband, will prove again the most successful bond over the failures of feminism and the fruitlessness of children, especially boys, becoming the criminals' toys.

And although you will inevitably be bewildered by the fast-moving pace of the changes happening to men in our society today, most of which are for worse rather than for better, one thing that you will have discovered from your life with your wife is that she is very wise, tries and often cries when crises arise. Women are very wise, very knowledgeable, and sometimes, wiser than us men, but she is not meant to be head of the family government.

They also know how to get their way. So it won't necessarily mean harm for you to take her word for it. Believe it or not, she often knows what's best for you. And I am sure that you know of events that have proved that to be true.

Me, Myself, and I

Changes to the detriment of men and for the advancement of women are taking shape more quickly than anyone can control. As a result, events are controlling our families more and more than the other way around, as women put careers before their children and their husbands.

As women alienate themselves from men more and more in pursuit of material things, men have become more and more frustrated with their wives. Women are more and more tired and grumpy and complain about everything that their husbands do or fail to do in the house.

They are now so tired and overworked that they have little or no time for their husbands. There is no time to cook, no time to eat together, no time to be together, no time for sex, and no time to talk. But there is a lot of time to argue and a lot of time to get snowed under with the burdens of everyday life. This is one of many good reasons why men are meant to be in charge of the family garage.

Her man gets fed every day with a daily dose of fault-finding such as, 'You are no good in the house. You are no good with the children. Where are you when I need you? I am the one doing all the work. You are stupid. You are an idiot. The kids and I are better off on our own than with you. I am too tired for sex. I need some "me" time. What have you done for me lately? I have no time for a kiss and a cuddle. Can't you see I am doing something? I get more response from the baby than from you. You are selfish. You only think about yourself, what about me?'

Women often make it look like they care for the whole family, when, in fact, they are being very selfish by referring to 'I' and 'me' nearly all the time. By putting everything else before their man, such as holding grudges for a long time, staying angry, man-hating tendencies, nagging, complaining, emotional manipulation, controlling through hurt, they are effectively sidelining him.

To 'relish life with the spouse you love each day and every day', (139), you must re-examine your thinking. Every marriage is made up of two flawed people. It's not that we don't know this, it's that we keep forgetting it, or hoping we are the exception to the rule. Expecting perfection is naïve and will keep undermining your relationship.

Happiness in marriage depends on coming to terms with your mutual defects and dealing with them realistically. Recognise fiction; deal with facts—especially in certain vulnerable areas. Self-focus, manipulation and demanding your way can never match God's unfailing system: 'Give, and it shall be given unto you . . .' 140.

You are given two eyes, two ears, two nostrils, but one mouth, one heart and one brain. Do more listening and more observing. Smell the goodness of the Lord and know that He is good. Put a guard over your mouth, protect your heart from the issues of life and stop behaving as if you have got more than one brain . . . . Be swift to hear, slow to speak, slow to wrath. 114. Do not be rash with your mouth, And let not your heart utter anything hastily before God. For God is in heaven, and you on earth; Therefore let your words be few. For a dream comes through much activity, And a fool's voice is known by his many words. 115.

Because if you keep telling him negative things day in day out, month in month out, and year in year out, eventually, he will start getting depressed and believe he is an idiot and worth nothing. You will have made him so depleted, physically and emotionally, that he will start feeling unwanted and not needed. How is that anyway to get the best out of your man, is what I say.

Putting your man down every day is the best way to get him down and drive him into the arms of someone else. You may be trying to get the best out of him, but, in fact, you will achieve the opposite thing. Women love to talk things to death, without coming to a conclusion or solving anything. You just love to talk, no matter what the consequences are. And that's one of the surest ways of seeing the death of your marriage, even if you are still living together.

Treat your man wisely—the way you would want to be treated yourself— and you will be shocked to see the changes in him. You will not believe it is the same man you were chastising. Give him what he wants, and you will be amazed to see the difference. A man is very a simple creature, not as complex as many women are. He does not ask for much, unlike his woman. All he asks for are four basic things in life: regular sex, his food, his clothes washed and being loved by his wife. Is that too much to ask for the vows you took at the altar?

Make your man happy with these four things, and you will get fourfold in return. You will get more than you thought was possible. You are his inspiration, the rock that he builds his home with. If that rock is solidly behind him, your family will do wonderful things. But if it is weak and worn, it will wear and ultimately tear him down.

Even when you are weak and worn and tear him down every day, he will still tell you that he loves you. He will still buy you flowers; he will still go to work to put food on the table. Even when you deny him sex time and time again, he will stay faithful most times. He will soldier on with the hope of better days ahead.

Why not make those days better for you two and not just seek for yourself and the children? When you look out for yourself and the children only, you will never be happy. Look out for the whole family, and you will be surprised how happy you will become.

Make him your best friend again, because he was there before the children and will be there when they are gone. There are times when you are going to need each other to pick up the pieces when no one else is around. If he is gone, you are going to wish your husband was there to help or even save your life one day. Wives, submit to your husbands, as to the Lord. For the husband is the head of the wife, . . . 15.

But unfortunately, the feminist movement backed by politicians have turned this long-standing and successful rule of the Bible on its head, with devastating consequences for husbands and children especially.

Survey after survey have shown that no one has benefited from the changes in the family structure in this country, and now Britain is the worst country in the developed world for family breakdowns and for bringing up children.

Though most people will not accept it, if one goes against the Word of God, you are bound to end up with failure or something less than ideal. So, men, 'The discretion of a man makes him slow to anger, And his glory is to overlook a transgression. 16. By pride comes nothing but strife, But with the well-advised is wisdom. 17. The beginning of strife is like releasing water; therefore stop contention before a quarrel starts. 18. See then that you walk circumspectly, not as fools, but as wise, redeeming the time, because *the days are evil*. Therefore do not be unwise, but understand what the perfect will of the Lord is. 19.

He who guards his mouth preserves his life, But he who opens wide his lips shall have destruction. 20. A soft answer turns away wrath, But a harsh word stirs up anger. The tongue of the wise uses knowledge rightly, But the mouth of the fool pours forth foolishness. 21.

So men, when your wife kicks off, even though it cuts and it hurts, keep your trap from opening, as you will only make the wound worse. You will invariably open a Pandora's box that you will not be able to control, because the moment you open your mouth she will step up a gear. The more you argue, the more frustrated you will become, because she counters every argument masterfully and with attacks of her own; she is often far ahead of you.

Some men end up resorting to violence when failure sets in. But this is not the way forward. Violence breeds violence and more and more resentment. The wise woman builds her house, But the foolish pulls it down with her hands. 22. In the mouth of a fool is the rod of pride, But the lips of the wise will preserve them. 23.

So keep your peace and keep your trap and your pent-up frustrations will only be short-lived. You know as much as I do that doing the opposite will only make matters far worse.

I know it is hard for us men, because women hold on to issues for a very long time and some hold on to them for their entire life. When a man just wants to let things go and forget about it, his wife keeps reminding him of his failures. So it is difficult to ignore. But ignore you must. That is the best way to allow things to die.

When she sees time and time again that you have no interest in arguing, she will, in most cases, let go. She will find new things to argue about. So try not to give her the pretext to argue in the first place, as she is, in most cases, more interested in being right than to show love and understanding to the most important man in her life.

Showing love all the time brings with it more and more appreciation and love in return. Thus breeding more and more happiness and satisfaction. But trying to prove the same point over and over again only breeds more and more resentment and pent-up frustrations. Yet we find that in families today everyone is trying to be right more and more than showing love, understanding, and forgiveness, which is becoming in shorter and shorter supply.

Often, the man is so shocked, taken aback, and bewildered by his wife's outbursts that he has no reply of his own. And if he comes up with one, it's often feeble and useless compared to his wife's polished and efficient verbal missile, designed to dismantle, demolish, and even destroy. We know this because many men drown their sorrows in things such as drink and drugs, while others go to the extreme of taking their own lives.

But, men, you must endure and have patience . . . count it all joy when you fall into various trials, knowing that the testing of your faith produces patience. But let patience have its perfect work, that you may be perfect and complete, lacking nothing. 24.

Divorce

ivorce or separation is not the answer either, as the woman usually ends up the victor. A separated or divorced man, when he thinks his problems are over, soon realises that they are just about to get worse and a lot worse. God did not make man to live on his own. That is why he created Eve for his company.

When a man goes to live on his own, his mental and physical health often deteriorates. When he goes to live with another woman, he soon realises that despite her faults, he was better off with his first wife and that he has jumped from the frying pan straight into the fire. He carries his unresolved faults and baggage from his first relationship into his new relationship, and before long, he wants to go back to his first wife. But often it is too late, and his life is unravelling before his very eyes. So if you know what's good for you, stay put—put up, and shut up. Some form of stability is better than instability. Blessed is the man that endures temptation . . . let every man be swift to hear, slow to speak, slow to wrath. 25.

Despite what you find yourself in, love your wife as you love yourself. The more she hurts you, the more you should love her. This is the best way forward, and it will work out for the benefit of both of you in the end.

You will do well to remember that the tongue cannot be tamed. Many have tried to tame the tongue and failed. Even as the tongue is a little member and boasts great things. See how great a forest a little fire kindles! And the tongue is a fire, a world of iniquity. The tongue is so set among our members that it defiles the whole body, and sets on fire the course of nature; and it is set on fire by hell. For every kind of beast and bird, of reptile and creature of the sea, is tamed and has been tamed by mankind. But no man can tame the tongue. It is an unruly evil, full of deadly poison. 26.

Be . . . pure, then peaceable, gentle, *willing to yield*, full of mercy and good fruits, without partiality and without hypocrisy. Now the fruit of righteousness is sown in peace, *by those who make peace.* 27.

Today's Reality—So Scary It's 'Not' Real

*O*ne of the most important starting points in life is to be oneself. We start doing that from birth when we develop our own personalities through the early years to become who we are by the time we are adults. Or so we think.

We may think that we have a personality all of our own making or our God-given personality. But if we think a little deeper, that it is not exactly true. Each of our personalities, especially in our early years is shaped by influences around us, most of which we have little or no control over, such as the influences coming from our parents.

Our parents, or lack of them, play a very large part in who we are and the type of people we become when they are no longer around. Our teachers' influence also plays a big part in shaping our personality.

Their influence, or lack of it, can be greater than we think: not only educationally with the knowledge they impart, but also their advice on matters that affect each individual; the punishment given to us for our misdemeanours, or the compliments paid when we do well; and the varied support or the extra mile they go for us in times of need.

The way others close to us conduct themselves around us also serves to influence the type of persons we become, often without us even realising it.

Then there are the outside influences, which force their way into our lives, such as television. Many would say that television serves a greater bad than good, which is partly the reason some parents do not allow televisions in their homes, while others do not permit it in their children's bedroom. Others have strict control over what their children watch and when. On the other hand, the opposite is true for others: some parents allow little or no control over what their children watch and the time of day or night that they watch it.

Most of us recognise the influences of television on young lives, but some are more concerned of their effects than others, hence the difference in approaches and outcomes.

There is also the influence of drink or drugs. Alcohol can make us, among other things, violent or depressed or act out of character; often to the despair of those we love.

I could go on and on about things or factors that help to shape our personality. But the point I wish to make about our personality is that it is shaped largely by factors we initially have little or no control over, because it is shaped from a very early age. Crucially, our personality will eventually benefit or be a detriment to those we come into contact with, as a result of the forces that helped to shape it.

In this chapter I want focus on parent—children relationship and the resultant personalities. In today's society these resultant personalities can be summed up in part by the Apostle Timothy.

He tells us plainly about these times . . . in the last days perilous times will come. For men will be lovers of themselves, lovers of money, boasters, proud, blasphemers, disobedient to parents, unthankful, unholy, unloving, unforgiving, slanderers, without self-control, brutal, despisers of good, traitors, headstrong, haughty, lovers of pleasure rather than lovers of God, having a form of godliness but denying its power. And from such people turn away. 28.

The Bible is certainly right here, as we live in an age where good human relations are valued less and less, while on the other hand, money and material possessions are valued more and more. So in today's world money and what it can buy is seen increasingly as more important than how we get along with each other. This invariably leads to more and more conflicts in the home, leading to a lot of single parenthood, resulting in the social breakdown we see in today's society.

As I alluded to before, the husband in the home is under severe attack. Now as a father, too, he is under attack. In a society where husbands and fathers are not valued any more, the father is under attack, first from his wife, then backed up by their children, then in a chain leading to the very politicians that have marginalised husbands and fathers in their legislations and speeches.

Firstly, women are resorting to violence against their husbands like never before and then they are backed up by their children, who now don't think twice about assaulting their father and their mothers, too. Children slap, push, punch and use household implements on their fathers, sometimes drawing blood in the process. Then if the man complains to the police, he is not taken seriously but is arrested himself, instead. This is what feminism and New Labour government policy have brought us to.

In today's world, husbands and fathers find themselves in a no-win situation. Some find that they have no choice but to leave the family home, and in total despair, some even resort to the most extreme measure of taking their own lives. Things have never been so bad for men in the home, and things do not look like getting any better in the short term, as government policies make it quite plain that not much is thought of our male folks today.

The tax credit system, for instance, which is designed to help poor families and lift them out of the poverty trap, is paid primarily to the mother to support her children. So whereas the mother does not often go out to work, this system sets in stone her stay-at-home position, whereby she only has to work part-time to reap the government windfall; while the husband, who normally works full-time plus the odd overtime, ends up taking home less than his wife, while having the bigger chunk of the household bills to pay. This cannot be fair and it is not.

In addition, should the marriage break up, she is guaranteed a further government windfall for becoming a single mother. Many take this encouragement to be a single mother seriously, while the man is left to fend for himself in nearly every sense. After a decade of this reckless policy, there are those who think that it is fair.

But the proof is in the pudding of the type of society we have ended up with. Despite these changes, which many feminists and their sympathisers think is fair, we have ended up with the worst social cohesion in Western Europe and in the Western world as a whole—so much for bringing about a 'fairer' society and a new era of 'progress'.

This seems more like an agenda, and someone who has an axe to grind wielding that axe. As I see it, women who have been kept back and held down for so long are now subtly taking their revenge on the male species in our society.

When we see that parents can no longer discipline their children with the rod, but we find instead that children are screaming and shouting obscenities at their father with the tacit support of their mother who hurls abuse of her own, you know that something is wrong with the society we live in.

No longer does the mother say, 'My child, you are wrong to speak to your father that way.' But instead, she weighs in with support of her own. Put succinctly, a man's wife sometimes does not know how to show love to her husband, as she was not shown love herself by her father when she was growing up. In addition, parents can no longer ask their children to do what they want them to do. The children know that they do not have to do what their parents ask them to, so they are openly disobedient, at nearly every turn.

Children have become very clever. They study their parents and the new system we live in very carefully to see what they can get away with, such as smoking, sex, drinking and even a pornographic film. And once you give them an inch, they often take a yard, and soon that yard becomes a mile, then ten miles and further and further. This scenario is figurative, as well as literal, and in many homes children are out of control.

Instead of obeying their parents, children are now trying to order their parents around, telling their parents what they should be doing for them, instead. Parent-children relationship, particularly in poorer families, where government policies have their greatest effect, is now a sad and sordid affair, with nothing in the past to compare.

Children have moved a step further also. Not only are they verbally abusing their parents, they are also now resorting to violence against their mothers and fathers, partly because they know that the law supports them over their parents in any conflict.

Should the parents call the police, alleging violence by their children against them, the parents are far more likely to be arrested, as all it takes is one lie from the child for the handcuffs to go on the parents. And when I say parent here, I mean the father, because in today's socialist and feminist society, the father, being beaten by his children or his wife, is seen as so ridiculous it's not worth pursuing.

If he calls the police, he is the one far more likely to be arrested. The law sympathises with mothers and children, to the detriment of fathers and his entitlements. Even more detrimental is that the onus is on the man only to prove his innocence. The mother and the children have nothing to prove and so they intrude on the father's plight, who with fright take flight. With current law and resulting conditions as they are, there is no incentive for fathers and husbands to stand firm and be attentive to the family firm, as women are the authorities only concern.

The children, knowing that they will get away with violence in the home, have taken their violence to their teachers in schools as well. In the west of England, for instance, nearly one in twenty children are suspended or expelled from secondary schools for bad behaviour each year. That is an astonishing figure. But that's what socialism, liberalism and feminism have brought us to. It's only a matter of time before another teacher gets killed or seriously injured in our schools again.

Not only do children disrespect their parents and their teachers, they also now disrespect the law and the keepers of the law—the police. Many of them try to fight pitched battles with the police also.

So let's reinforce what the Bible has to say about these times once more . . . in the last days perilous times will come. For men will be lovers of themselves, lovers of money, boasters, proud, blasphemers, disobedient to parents, unthankful, unholy, unloving, unforgiving, slanderers, without self-control, brutal, despisers of good, traitors, headstrong, haughty, lovers of pleasure rather than lovers of God, having a form of godliness but denying its power. 29.

In days gone by, when a parent talked to his or her child sternly, a sense of respect and fear of punishment would come over that child, causing him or her to know his or her place, with a sense of right and wrong and behave accordingly. In addition, when a parent spoke, he or she would get the support of his or her partner to reinforce what is right, what is acceptable and what is not, and who is in charge.

That fear and respect is now gone. Now when a parent talks to his or her child, that unity between parents is often not there any more, and with the support of one parent over the other, that child seizes the opportunity to gain the upper hand over the hapless parent. Like someone acting out of greed, the child burrows for more and more gain to see what else he or she can get away with. And the less control the parents show over the child, the more the child pushes the boundaries of acceptability. This scenario is made worse when the parents are divided. Divide and rule takes shape with the children or the teenage child starting to take over.

So, for instance, children are now telling parents to shut up instead of the other way around. Children are now calling their parents all sorts of derogatory names and shouting obscenities at them at the top of their voices. This would not have been dreamed of even a decade ago. Children are now shouting at their parents at the same level that parents used to shout at their children several years ago.

Children are now ridiculing their parents even in front of their friends. The shocked parents now huddle in a corner, bewildered at the turn of events in our society today. And if that is not enough, children are now hitting their parents, often drawing blood in the process.

What have you learnt from your life with Lucifer? Surely it was a life of loses and strife, of illnesses and diseases that displeases and grieves your soul as you grow rapidly old. Who wants to grow rapidly old? You have let the Devil in who is now giving you, with glee, the grave, which you can still boldly flee.

Just look at me. I Bless the Lord, O my soul, And forget not all His benefits: Who forgives all my iniquities, because I fled the Devil and would not level with his deadly deeds. Who heals all my diseases, who redeems my life from destruction, Who crowns me with loving kindness and tender mercies, Who satisfies my mouth with good things, So that my youth is renewed like the eagle's. Psalms 103:2-5.

So why not go for the youthful thing instead of going for glasses of wine or a bottle of gin, which makes your liver meaner and harder, so does not recover. Get over your life of sin, pain and suffering, rapid ageing and unhealthy living, by doing the youthful thing which is the bible that blows your past into oblivion with a blast. Thus reviving your life into glory and spice, bringing you much needed health, spiritual wealth and a big surprise.

Survive Satan and sin. Get God and put on a grin with the knowledge that you managed to break free from sicknesses, suffering and pain, and now you have everything to gain, by making plain you are looking ahead for your eternal bread, forgetting those things which are behind and reaching forward to those things which are ahead. I press toward the goal for the prize of the upward call of God in Christ Jesus. Because my God shall supply all your needs according to His riches in glory by Christ Jesus. Now to our God and Father be glory forever and ever. Amen. Philippians 3:13,14,19.

What a wonderful joy when you forget your life of sin and crime, and put it all behind; A joy when you have found the One that is fun, solid and sound; One who will never fail you once He is found. One that is not shy to lift you from your filth and make you fly; One who will share all your joys as well as your sufferings when you give them all to Him. One who will take all your pain without fail. And give gain that wipes away all your stain.

One who makes plain you are loved with an everlasting love from above. A love that's sure and pure, and pours out forever more; A love that's one of a kind that you will never find from one of your kind; A love so close He comes with a purpose to give you a surplus of health, spiritual wealth and everything else that Christ bled and died for when He became the one, true and only risen Saviour.

Therefore humble yourselves under the mighty hand of God, that He may exalt you in due time, casting all your care upon Him, for He cares for you.

But, Be sober, be vigilant; because your adversary the devil walks about like a roaring lion, seeking whom he may devour. Resist him, steadfast in the faith, knowing that the same suffering are experienced by your brotherhood in the world.

But may the God of all grace, who called us to His eternal glory by Christ Jesus, after you have suffered a while, perfect, establish, strengthen, and settle you.

To Him be the glory and the dominion for ever and ever. Amen. 1 Peter 5:6-11.

Be strong, therefore, and strive to overcome, and become what the Son desires for you, which is not to become a stew to the heat of the midnight street, with its filth complete. But to draw near even when you are bare, and feel His loving embrace, which in this world is too often false and scarce.

Fathers are being kicked, punched spat on and every household implement including stiletto shoes and knives are being used on them, by their children as well as by their female partners and wives. From the injuries sustained, some of them life threatening, many fathers end up in hospital for treatment. Others resort to fighting back, landing themselves in trouble with the law. While others think that this life, in its present form, is not worth it and so take their own lives. Under New Labour suicide rates among fathers have risen alarmingly, so have suicides among children.

And the father who finds himself under any form of physical attack, no matter how serious, dare not touch his or her child, because even while being pilloried and damaged from the blows of his own child, he knows that should he lift a finger in self-defence, he is likely to go to jail or even to prison.

As a father in this day and age, one should not get involved, . . . And have no fellowship with the unfruitful works of darkness, but rather expose them. 40.

Some children resort to taking their own lives because they come to realise that the treatment they have been meeting out to their parents is unacceptable, and so the guilt of it all has served to destroy them.

The latest talk I hear from the liberal and the feminist movement, is about children being allowed to sue their parents over various issues to do with their parenting, once they grow up. What a state of madness and stupidity we have come to in this country!

This state of sad affairs where the children have just about taken over the home and some are looking to take over their schools and their neighbourhoods is more prevalent in non-Christian homes than it is in God-fearing homes. These are homes where there are loose morals or little or no morals at all.

Also in upper-income-strata homes, this state of affairs is less prevalent for various reasons. Some of the reasons are that there are less marital breakdowns, so in most cases, the traditional family is still intact, whereby the husband and father is the main breadwinner; hence he remains the head of the household.

Another reason is that there is less reliance on the government and its benefit system and more reliance on Christian values in many cases.

As a result, the children in these homes have more respect for their parents, their teachers, and their elders in general. They also do better in schools than their poorer counterparts. To maintain and improve their more successful way of life, they prefer that their children not be educated in the public sector. One of the reasons for disliking the public sector is that more affluent parents do not want the influences of unruly children to rub off on their children.

Ironically, poorer families want their children to be educated alongside richer children, while at the same time abandoning the traditional family way of life, which most affluent parents aspire to, simply because of its proven success. More recently, however, poorer families have been coming back round to the same thinking of more affluent families, as surveys show that 49% of parents and 19% of pupils now think that corporal punishment should be reintroduced in schools for very bad behavior.

There is too much experimentation going on with the abandonment of the traditional family, and it is producing nothing but failure, hence a bigger than necessary strain on government services—the very government that put these experimental changes in place in the first place.

Don't you know that experimenting with life, brings with it a flavour of strife, stress and regress into madness! Then the combustible mess created is too much for anyone to redress. Experimenting is a process of learning. There is no solidity or foundation to build a stable nation. So what stupidity when you put your trust in frivolity.

In these homes where government experimentation ignites an already bad situation, children are allowed to do things such as smoke cigarettes and even drugs by their own parents. At the same time, the laws on drugs were slackened, presumably to allow greater drug use. Children are allowed to drink alcohol by parents, even though the law forbids it. Children are allowed by their parents to indulge in illicit sex with their peers even in the family home, by not stopping them and educating them in the rights, wrongs, and pitfalls here. Children being allowed to talk to anyone they please on the Internet has become a disease. And if that is not enough of a disaster they are also allowed to watch television with sexual and violent contents with their young lover, even after the midnight hour. Yet they want the same education, achievements, and results of more affluent families.

Restraining ourselves—self-control—is listed in the bible as proof God's Spirit lives within us. 116. Living without restraint is like removing the brakes from your car. It may be exciting for a while, but inevitably you'll pay a high price for the ride. Take away the brakes, and your life, like your car, is transformed into an unguided missile headed for disaster.

It's impossible to live a lifestyle of moral purity without dealing with some practical facts related to our flesh-and-blood appetites that constantly crave satisfaction. The bible says, 'Do not let sin control the way you live; do not give in to sinful desires. Do not let any part of your body become an instrument of evil to serve sin.

Instead, give yourselves completely to God . . . realise that . . . whatever you choose to obey . . . (becomes your master)' 117. If you let it, your body will lead you off course. It isn't that your body is evil; it's just that it possesses a number of appetites that are always ready to respond to the surrounding stimuli, all of which are terribly appealing and temporarily satisfying.

One bible scholar writes: 'Life on earth is really nothing more than a string of moments, one after another. And I do not want my testimony for Jesus Christ to be shattered by a single moment of indulging my flesh. I don't want one moment of rage or pride or lust to cast a shadow over a lifetime of walking with the Lord. Frankly, I fear that possibility. And do you know what? I want to fear that possibility. When I stop fearing it, I'm in grave danger.

Our values today are badly messed up. How about 'celebrity justice?' Someone famous gets a free pass, while the less fortunate do time because they did the crime? Wrong! We need to teach our children that unless they accept responsibility, they will live unsuccessfully: 'A man reaps what he sows.' So either God's word will keep you away from sin or sin will keep you away from God's word.

So, parent, taking personal responsibility means holding your child accountable when they violate the rules, mix with the wrong crowd; try 'cool' stuff like drinking, drugs and premarital sex; cheat on test; or stay out beyond curfew. Sound straight laced? So is gravity. So is the harvest law.

Your sincere but naïve sentiment, 'I want them to have all the things I didn't have growing up,' will turn spoiled children into spoiled adults. Practice prevention: build a fence at the top of the cliff, not a hospital at the bottom!

You say, 'By the time I get home at night I'm too tired to discipline them.' Wake up: When they get arrested for drink driving the judge won't cut them any slack. When they get killed in a car crash, you will hold yourself guilty for not seeing to it that your son was brought up properly.

The bank won't cut them any slack either when they repossess their car and their house because they did not pay the amount due. Kindness is cruelty in disguise when it's not accompanied by responsibility.

Eli the High Priest rose to the top of his profession. Only one problem, he did not take responsibility for his family. As a result, he and his son died prematurely. God says, 'I told him that I would judge his family … because … he failed to restrain them' 113. So, take responsibility! (**Source: UCB's The Word for Today**).

Some of the liberal policy-making government members don't even send their children to schools in the public sector. Some send their children to church schools, obviously for the values that these institutions bring to bear and their resulting success.

Yet their policies of madness towards societies best, even toward church schools, and Christianity in general would make us all a mess in the pit of political 'progress'. They hate Christianity, but ironically they seem to hate their own public sector schools even more when it comes to their own children.

They despise the public sector when it comes to their own children. They can't bear the thought of having their children being brought up with children of the working class and the values that they might bring to bear—values, as they well know, and which everyone can see, are the product of their misguided and deluded policies.

It makes one wonder if they are truly liberally minded, or is it that they want one rule for the poor and one rule for the rich, including themselves. After all, a lot of their policies, the ones that work, are stolen from the conservative right.

I have already mentioned that if one goes against the teaching of the Bible, one is bound to end up with failure or something less than ideal. And that is exactly what we are finding with families, especially poorer families.

So this is what the Bible says about older men and women who are often the heads of families. But as for you, speak the things that are proper for sound doctrine, that the older men be sober, reverent, temperate, sound in faith, in love, in patience; the older women likewise, that they be reverent in behaviour, not slanderers, not given to much wine, teachers of good things, that they admonish the young women to love their husbands, to love their children, to be discreet, chaste, homemakers, good, obedient to their husbands, that the word of God may not be blasphemed. Likewise, exhort the young men to be sober-minded, In all things showing yourself to be a pattern of good works; in doctrine showing integrity, reverence, incorruptibility, sound speech that cannot be condemned, the one who is an opponent be ashamed having nothing evil to say of you. 30.

And as for children or subordinates: Remind them to be subject to rulers and authorities, to obey, to be ready for every good work, to speak evil of no one, to be peaceable, gentle, showing all humility to all men. For we ourselves were also once foolish, disobedient, deceived, serving various lusts and pleasures, living in malice and envy, hateful and hating one another. 31.

Children obey your parents in the Lord for this is right. "Honour your father and mother," which is the first commandment and promise, that it may be well with you and you may live long on the earth. And you, fathers, do not provoke your children to wrath, but bring them up in the training and admonition of the Lord. 32.

For families this is the sound advice given: . . . with all lowliness and gentleness, with long-suffering, bearing with one another in love, endeavouring to keep the unity of the Spirit in the bond of peace. 33 . . . that we should no longer be children, tossed to and fro and carried about with every wind of doctrine, by trickery of men, in cunning craftiness of deceitful plotting, but speaking the truth in love, may grow up in all things into Him who is head—Christ. 34.

Let no corrupt word proceed out of your mouth, but what is good for necessary edification, that it may impart grace to the hearers. 35. But fornication and all uncleanness or covetousness, let it not be named among you . . . neither filthiness nor foolish talking, nor coarse gesturing, which are not fitting, but rather giving thanks. 36.

For husbands, here is more sound advice that cannot be ignored if one wants to achieve a successful relationship: So husbands ought to love their own wives as their own bodies; he who loves his wife loves himself. For no one ever hates his own flesh, but nourishes it and cherishes it, just as the Lord does the church. 37.

He who despises the word will be destroyed, But he who fears the command-ment will be rewarded. The law of the wise is a fountain of life, To turn one away from the snares of death. Good understanding gains favour, But the way of the unfaithful is hard. Every prudent man acts with knowledge, but a fool lays open his folly. 38.

We ignore these words to our detriment and our ultimate destruction. But that is exactly the direction families have been moving in, in the last thirteen years or so of socialist rule. And it has brought nothing but devastation to families, especially poorer families and the country as a whole.

So in building strong character, '(It is) better to have self-control than to conquer a city'. 118. First and foremost, building strong character requires self-discipline. Self-discipline is the ability to do what's right, when you don't feel like it. Plato asserted, 'The first and best victory is to conquer self.' Yes, your greatest victories are internal ones. Bobby Jones was winning golf tournaments by age 12. But he had a temper. His nickname was 'club-thrower'.

An older gentleman called grandpa Bart recognised Jones' talent and his character issues. He said, 'Bobby, you're good enough to win, but you'll never win big until you control that temper of yours.' Jones did master his temper, and went on to win his first U.S. Open at 21. Grandpa Bart used to say, 'Bobby was 14 when he mastered golf, but he was 21 when he mastered himself.'

English theologian Henry Parry Liddon observed, 'What we do on some great occasion will probably depend on what we already are; and what we are will be the result of previous years of self-discipline.'

If you're serious about building strong character, set higher standards for yourself and refuse to lower them. Need a role model? You won't find a better one than Jesus. He said, 'If anyone would come after me, he must deny himself' 119. Each day look for an opportunity to say 'no' to yourself in some small area. Try it; you'll be surprised how hard it is. But the payoff will come when you need to say no to yourself in some big area of your life. Like saving for a rainy day, you'll have spiritual strength to draw on when you need it. **(Source: UCB's The Word for Today).**

Fruits of Policy-maker New Labour

The left agenda seeks to take away some of the child's rights including his or her right to know his or her rightful father, thus bowing further to the feminist agenda.

The terms 'husband' and 'wife' have been removed from nearly every, if not, every government form that now exists. These terms have been replaced with the term 'partner'—a nod to feminism and a further nail in coffin of the traditional family.

Make no mistake about it; women do a very good job at bringing up children. They may even do a better job than men, on their own. But everyone, including the feminist, knows that two parents—a husband and a wife—do a far better job than a common law relationship or single parents.

So one can't see the reason for the headstrong rush to destroy the traditional family, except someone may have an axe to grind against men in general.

Women are meant to be at their best for children between birth and about twelve years of age. That is when children need their mothers most. Boys, especially, need their fathers most in their teenage years. Then, the father can guide his son to become a successful man, and he can be a good example for his son to follow. The father also plays the role of the main disciplinarian, keeping his son out of trouble.

Boys have more respect for both parents bringing them up, than they have for the 'weaker' sex—the mother—trying to play the role of mother and father. And this is where the single-parent families' failures are at their greatest.

Things are also often made worse when a single mother takes in another man, who is not the children's father. Her teenage sons and daughters quite often lose respect for their mother and have little or none for the new man in their life, either. There is no excuse for this, but this is the reality in Britain today. In addition, the children may feel left out as they now think that their mother is paying more attention to the new lover in her life.

Boys who have not got their natural father at home or a father who has been so drummed down by his mother's tongue that he has become nothing more than a figurehead, tend to look elsewhere for male role models. And they usually find it in the wrong forms such as their peers, who sometimes get them into trouble with their indulgence in drugs, violence, sex, or alcohol.

Boys in particular get involved with drink, drugs, and violence at an early age. Soon they become hooked, and the single mother loses all control of her child. Next, the police become involved when all else fails, and her once-lovely, but now-lost son, becomes a part of the criminal justice system. He starts off with the Acceptable Behaviour Order—ABS or 'Area of Basic Schooling'; then the Antisocial Behaviour Order—ASBO, or 'Advanced Schooled Behaviour into Oblivion'. If and when these fail, he graduates to his first prison sentence.

Once again, our country breaks records for the number of young people that it sends to prisons.

Another area that children get lost in is the Internet. With little or no supervision from parents, children, who are often very naive, speak to all types of people, some of whom are downright dangerous. According to many surveys done, a staggering figure of one in seven children have admitted to chatting with strangers on the Internet. Children even give out their personal details to total strangers, many of whom are only interested in fulfilling their own sexual desires and destroying a young life.

Children live what they learn and learn what they live very quickly. These days, the mum has a much bigger influence than the dad in the home. And one of the things that children are learning, and learning fast, is that as the government destroys the traditional family, (and some mothers, taking their cue from the government and other feminists, do it as well by constantly tongue-lashing the husbands), it is all right for them to do it also. To make matters worse, the mother often does not object to what and how her children speak to their dad, so he finds his role as a dad diminished more and more with each passing day.

Many mothers in poorer families are themselves the product of a broken home and the product of a very sinful lifestyle, whereby they too were brought up by a single mother, and see all kinds of immorality including sexual immorality around them. So they do not appear to know how to treat the father of their children, hence the true value of him. Therefore, they find history repeating itself, in that, their family heads in the same direction their mother's family went. The only difference is that they often find that their scenario is worse than the one they grew up in, as these days are far more evil.

The politicians responsible for dismantling the traditional family are only too aware of the results of their policies, but they seem determined to press further along regardless.

Men and Women

The role of the husbands is eroded further in today's society as women go after career goals, putting children second and spouses third. The husband can now be called 'modern man' if he can take over the housekeeping—such cleaning the house, cooking the meal, and looking after the children—to please a wife that he hardly ever sees because she is always out working or at college or university or with friends. And when they do see each other, she is too tired to make love to her husband. At the same time, he has a job, so he too hardly ever sees his wife, all in the name of 'progress, change, and modernisation.'

But as we all know, there is little or no happiness in this type of life. In addition, love is eroded as there is little or no relationship left between husband and wife. They become society's conveyer belt for the payment of bills. This scenario of greed breeds more and more unhappiness, often leading to illicit relationships being formed with others and infidelity. This then leads to the break-up of marriages, turning what is usually a bad financial situation, any way, into a crisis. My son . . . do not associate with those given to change, for their calamity will rise suddenly, and who knows the ruin those two can bring. 39.

The biggest losers in this situation are nearly always the children, who will now be brought up in a broken home. After thirteen years or so of socialist rule, this is what 'modernisation,' 'progress', and 'change' have brought our society. We now have more debt and broken homes than any other Western country.

Husbands and wives have been for some time doing two jobs, even three jobs each, to try and balance the books. But after a decade or more of this type of life, or more accurately put—this type of existence, things for most families have gotten worse rather than better.

The current scenario of putting material gain before the family is now proving insane, and has seen a record number of families seeking debt advice from the citizens' advice bureau, a record number of families entering into a voluntary financial arrangement with their creditors, and a record number of people filing for bankruptcy.

The toll on families, especially children, is incalculable, but these scenarios are entirely predictable because as a Christian, one knows, as a matter of fact, that society is headed in the wrong direction.

Despite over ten years of socialist rule, whereby wealth should be redistributed, there are more families than ever before living below the poverty line. In Britain, there are families that can hardly afford an evening meal each day of the week. There are more children on free school meals than ever before. Instead of putting food on the table, many families find that their first priority is to try to grapple with the debt mountain that they find themselves in. As a result, not only are children going to bed without a proper meal, but also their diet has become increasingly poor, as families can afford to buy only the cheapest food available or not afford food at all anymore.

The more families struggle with their financial situation, the worse things get, as the option of doing another job does not exist. This is because many husbands and wives are already doing two jobs each.

And as their financial situation gets worse, the family bickers more and more, so driving things into reverse. Advice and counselling services for husbands, wives, and families in general have never been so busy. With five million divorcees, we are once again breaking unwanted records in Europe and the Western world in general.

As the feminist agenda takes precedence in our society, women no longer think it cool to be feminine. No longer do many women please their husbands and stay at home to look after the children.

Women think themselves as superior and now play the roles of a man and a woman in the house. They have become more and more aggressive and more and more masculine. So the man in the house is tongue-lashed frequently about how 'bad' or 'useless' he is. The man is even told that he is inferior and not in the same league as women.

Men are denied their very being these days and are made to feel that it is not good or cool to be a man anymore. While being made to feel inferior, ironically, we are told that men and women are equal and that sameness should be promoted.

SCRIPTURAL FORTIFIERS

'HE IS ABLE TO HELP US WHEN WE ARE BEING TEMPTED.'
HEBREWS 2:18. NLT

If you are facing temptation today, here are 7 Scriptural fortifiers—use them!!!

a. 'The temptations that come into your life are no different from what others experience. And God is faithful. He will not allow temptation to be more than you can stand. When you are tempted, He will show you a way out so that you can endure' (1 Corinthians 10:13 NLT).

b. 'I give unto you power ... over all the power of the enemy: and nothing shall by any means hurt you' (Luke 10:19).

c. 'The God of peace will soon crush Satan under your feet … the grace, (strength and enablement) of our Lord Jesus be with you' (Romans 16:20 NLT).

d. 'Use every piece of God's armour, so you will be able to resist the enemy in the time of evil; so that after the battle you will still be standing firm' (Ephesians 6:13 NLT)

e. Don't be afraid for I am with you. Don't be dismayed, for I am your God. I will strengthen you. I will help you. I will hold you up with My victorious right hand' (Isaiah 41:10 NLT).

f. 'This High Priest of ours understands our weaknesses, for He faced all the same temptations we do, yet He did not sin. So let us come boldly to the throne of our gracious God. There we will receive His mercy, and we will find grace to help us when we need it' (Hebrews 4:15-16 NLT).

g. 'The Lord knows how to rescue godly people from their trials' (2 Peter 2:9 NLT). Sheep are wise; when the wolf comes they just move closer to the shepherd. The same goes for you! (Source: UCB's The Word for Today) When it matters to feminists, the differences between men and women do not exist and should not be flagged up, but sameness should be promoted, instead. For them male values and masculinity are seen as a threat, rather than be complimented with feminine qualities.

Females have become like men in many circumstances—no longer feminine and to be admired and loved by men—but instead, they have come to love, admire, and promote themselves to the detriment of their children and their menfolk. And with their gift of the gab, their menfolk are often meant to feel small and humiliated. Today men are even physically beaten by the woman in their lives as well as by their children.

Today femininity is about infidelity, free sex, immorality, abortion and abortion rights, binge drinking, smoking, being career-oriented, partying, and treating one's self. In short, it is all about 'I, me, myself, and what I can do and get for myself'. Also it is about doing everything that men do, because 'we are equal and can do anything a man can.' Variety and difference no longer exist or should not be promoted.

In addition, their men, if they do have one, are encouraged to get unto their agenda or get lost. And many men do try to be this modern man. But the truth is that he can never make the grade because despite all his efforts, many women are never happy or satisfied with the efforts of their men and allow their tongue to run before their heads. They are more concerned with being right all the time, rather than in showing love and understanding and being loved.

Another approach of women towards men in today's world is that they can do it all, and that they do not need a man or that a man is the least of all their needs in life today. They can be a mother, a father, do two jobs, do the DIY in the house, and last and least important are their husbands.

Day in, day out, husbands up and down in our country listen to their women as they make known what they think about them and what should be done with men in general. They are even told that, 'some men, and in some cases all men, should be castrated'. Men are told that they are, 'hopeless' or that they are, 'useless'. They are, 'not as good as women. Women are superior to men. Men need to stand on their own two feet and stop being propped up by their wives.' The 'hopeless' and 'useless' men are told to help their wives more and take on more of the housework. 'Men need to move with the times and become modern men.' 'Women do not need men.' 'What we need is a sperm bank for when we need children.' 'Men are immature and stupid.' These comments are sometimes aired publicly as well as among feminine groups. Yet men do not speak publicly about their women in this way.

In the current atmosphere, men have become timid and afraid to be men and fathers. Boys have become afraid to be boys, as they are constantly told that girls are better, and feminist issues are promoted over family issues.

Feminism has taught women that marriage, men, and children are oppressors and the real enemies of womanhood. They have brainwashed many of us into believing that men need women more than women need men or that women do not need men at all.

The truth of the matter is that men and women need each other equally. Single mothers are not coping very well at all, especially with their teenage boys, as the statistics show time and time again, and as we can see from our television news screens. Single men don't live very healthy or happy lives, either. They die younger, and single women are more likely to have a serious illness than if they lived with their husbands.

Women have become rough, tough, harsh, loud, loutish, sometimes downright rude, and altogether more masculine. As a result, men are finding women less attractive and more and more difficult to get along with. More and more women are losing their feminine attributes in the name of self-advancement, self-promotion, and promoting feminism at all cost.

The basic thesis of feminism is that a woman cannot advance herself by submitting to her husband. They go even further by suggesting that there is no life for women in marriage, let alone submitting to their husbands. They see marriage as oppression and slavery if the husband is the head, but not if the wife is the head, which is increasingly the case these days.

They say that men and women are equal, and so there should be two heads of the household, doing and sharing everything equally. But that line is just used as a prerequisite for taking over completely. Many women are not interested in equality because they think that they are superior to men.

In every matter concerning equality, women bond together in opposition to men. It is a favourite pastime of women to put men down these days, while men sit back, listen, and soak up all the insults thrown at them.

On a recent television programme, aired on ITV on Thursday, 10 January 2008, One woman was exalting women so much, while at the same time putting men down, that another woman on the same programme said, 'Aren't you "bigging" up women so much that you are in danger of becoming anti-men?' Of course she denied it, but the facts of life these days show otherwise and bear out the points that have been made in this book so far.

The point being attacked on the programme was men's competitiveness. By and large, a lot of men's competitiveness has been taken away from them, as they are discouraged from doing the things that they are best at and encouraged to be more like women. The husband is encouraged more and more to submit to the feminist agenda, giving his wife everything she wants, while his needs are constantly trampled on.

So today, a husband is not much of a man any more, but instead, he is an adjunct of his wife and her needs. That's what we call today a modern man. Modern man is a subject of his wife: a puppet to, 'she who must be obeyed'. He has become a crumple in the carpet to be trampled on at will to fill her fancy and egoistic incline to sin even while being drunk with a bottle of gin.

We all know that there is no chance of there being two heads of the household with each one sharing the responsibilities equally and crucially, having equal authority over the children for instance. It's just not possible. There is no other organisation that advocates this sort of a scenario, and so it does not exist anywhere.

In any society, there is one prime minister, not two; one queen or president, not two; in schools, there is one head teacher, not two, and so on.

Only in the home is this concept of two heads advocated; yet everyone knows that it does not and cannot work. But it is advocated less and less these days as women have now taken over the headship of the family, which is what they wanted in the first place.

They dare not say that, so they cover it up in the cloak of equality.

The war being waged by feminists to take over the family at all costs has caught men on the hop, as he is more concerned to work past seven o'clock leaving her to watch the clock. So she often devises a devious plan to make him pay for every last drop of time that he could, but did not spend with her and their lot, as he is instead focused on working till he drops.

And those that drop literally or find themselves being farmed out, will be congratulated by the next man in her life for leaving him with such an inheritance he could not hitherto have dreamed of or have worked for.

As a result, they have no idea of how to respond to a well-oiled machine backed by the government of the day.

So a husband, who is mainly interested in his meals, sex, his clothes being taken care of, providing for his family and just being loved generally, find himself fumbling and struggling to respond to this well-organised, but devious movement, that now has affairs at will and changes her man if she no longer fancies him. And with a little help from her friend, whose main interest is to wreak havoc on men, she knows that she has a destructive line to womankind in the midnight hour when her man is under cover trying to recover for work in the morning hour.

And in that midnight hour she and her friend gets up to all sorts including finding her a boyfriend, to subtly show her husband that he is no longer her friend, while sometimes pretending all is well, when in fact she is messing with his head and wishing he was dead.

With a lot of malign time wined and dined with her female friend and sometimes her boyfriend, she often attacks her husband instead of being his rock to defend to the end; thus putting a mar on, and being in rage with, the institution that saved the age from the financial, civil and criminal weight of the dysfunctional one parent family trait. This institution, is as we all know, is marriage!

And when she find being in bed with the man God sent too much to stomach, she finds solace instead in the hopelessness, disparaging and blasphemous sentiments of her friend, dressed up as good fun at the end of a phone line or in text messages sent in the midnight hour, like the following I found on my wife's phone, supposedly when I was all alone under my bed cover, preparing for work in the morning hour.

> "Lord, B4 I lay down 2 sleep, I pray 4 a man whos not a creep, One who's handsome, smart + strong, One who's willy is thick + long, Oh send me a man who makes love 2 my mind, Knows just what to say when I ask "how bigs my behind?" And as I kneel + pray by my bed, I look at the wanker u sent me instead. amen"

Abraham Lincoln said that it's better to keep your mouth shut and be thought a fool, than to open it and remove all doubt.

Every pleasure in our lives comes at a price. For the legitimate pleasures, we pay the price beforehand, with the pain of self-sacrifice. But for the illegitimate pleasures, we pay the price afterwards with the severe pain of seeing our lives, our health and our families going down the drain. But the greatest pleasure of all is serving the Lord God almighty by faith in His son Jesus Christ, who said through the apostle Paul: . . . have no fellowship with the unfruitful works of darkness, BUT RATHER EXPOSE THEM. For it is shameful even to speak of those things which are done by them in secret. But all things that are exposed are made manifest by the light, for whatever makes manifest is light. 40.

Everyone proud in heart is an abomination to the Lord; Though they join forces none will go unpunished. 41.

Before destruction the heart of a man is haughty, and before, honour is humility. 42.

He who walks with wise men will be wise, but the companion of fools will be destroyed. 43.

But those who rebuke the wicked will have delight, and a good blessing will come upon them. 44.

Generally speaking, there is no support for men out there once he is shown the door, while, on the other hand, the women in the house get all the support they need plus what they don't need from innumerable quarters. There are now so many organisations geared towards the support of women, it is truly amazing. There is no shortage of places for them to turn to in times of distress, while husbands struggle to find any support for their needs.

Even when there is support for both parties, quite often the end result is that the mediators support the wife's point of view and needs, to the detriment of the husband. Often when there is a female mediator, she is more inclined to support the views of the wife over the husband, instead of taking an objective line. In today's world women are far more united than men, and whenever there is a crisis, they tend to bind together, to the exclusion of and/ or destruction of men.

Many men eventually get kicked out of the house and end up with a relative, in a hostel, or on the streets. Today it is a pitiful sight to see the number of men in hostels and on the streets as beggars.

Men are quite simple creatures, not as complicated and sophisticated as women. So they like the basics above all else. And these are meals, sex, clothes, and being loved. But even these basics are difficult to gain for today's husbands. And these basics are becoming increasingly difficult to come by, as wives are more and more interested in themselves and their friends and less and less interested in their husbands and their children.

Husbands are now an endangered species that are disappearing fast in favour of single-parent families. And children are now disappearing from the female psyche in favour of being the career woman. And when it's time for children, some women prefer not to have children by a man, but instead by artificial insemination. Having a unanimous sperm donor is becoming fashionable.

Many women no longer want children or they'd rather have children in later life because they put their careers first. In every sphere of life, money now comes first, even in the home. But with a debt burden of £1.3 trillion in this country, a debt burden bigger than all the products and services produced in a year or about 120% of GDP, it's headed for tears in a matter of a few years and in many quarters. A staggering £95 billion alone is being paid in interest in one year before a penny of debt is paid back. With this scenario, we are certainly headed for a crisis of some sort, with a lot more broke and broken families to come. As expected, the children are expected to pick up the pieces for their parents' mistakes.

But it can all be avoided if we follow the words of the bible that says, the older women likewise, that they be reverent in behaviour, not slanderers, not given to much wine, teachers of good things, that they admonish the young women to love their husbands, to love their children, to be discreet, chaste, homemakers, good, obedient to their husbands, that the word of God may not be blasphemed. Likewise, exhort the young men to be sober-minded. In all things showing yourself to be a pattern of good works; in doctrine showing integrity, reverence, incorruptibility, sound speech that cannot be condemned, the one who is an opponent be ashamed having nothing evil to say of you. 45. Allow these wise words to take root as they once did, and one and all will benefit from wisdom and sanity, thus getting rid of the sordid filth that we as a nation have fallen neck-deep into, and which has put us firmly on the skids.

Change the Hard Way

*I*n some relationships, many of us think that things will never get better, but they can. If one party decides that whatever the cost, he or she is not going to get involved in a slanging match, you will at some stage start to notice change. It may not come in weeks or months or possibly a few years, but change for the better will come to your relationship, if you stick with it.

One of the easiest things to do is to walk away from a relationship when things are not going well, especially when one keeps getting put-down on how 'bad' and 'useless' one is and that one can never do anything right. It is very hard indeed, and it hurts deeply every time your spouse opens his or her mouth.

And you think that things will get better if you simply walk away. But as anyone who has been there will tell you, things are just about to become more complicated to the point of disaster. Everything that you least expected starts befalling you.

The feeling of 'missing the family' creeps in, so does loneliness and a sense of sadness and loss. You often think that by hooking up with someone new, your problems will go away. But you can be with someone new and still feel lonely.

Often times nothing except Christ can replace the first love in your life, and certainly nothing except Christ can replace a family.

So if you are having a problem in your relationship, remember that walking away will, in most cases, make matters worse rather than better. You should only leave if you are asked to. Then the other party will be left to realise how bad a decision that was. Things will start falling down around him or her quicker than one could conceivably imagine.

The problems with the children will probably be the most noticeable change. They will be very irritable and start misbehaving, as at least one of them will want his or her parent, usually the father, back.

Soon the lone parent finds that she spends more time trying to control her children than she would like. In many cases she finds that the situation is so out of control that some of the children, or at least one child, decide to go his or her own way. With the absence of a male role model in the house for instance, he or she often goes to find one outside. This then brings additional problems of its own, which are usually more than what a single parent can bear.

When one child rebels against his or her parents, the other children, who often worry about their wayward sibling, are left to pick up the pieces of lost childhood and a miserable life resulting.

So the partner, usually the woman who has put her husband out, is made to struggle a lot more than when her partner was around. And often, she refuses to see her own faults in the relationship, as she is always right, and so blames everything on her husband instead. To make matters worse for men, the authorities and the agencies involved with families have latched on to this one-sided approach. A word of advice—it takes two to tango.

Women, who are often heralded as being more sensible in the home, are not as wise as is being portrayed, as their tongue often goes before their heads, not to mention the mood swings caused by their monthly cycle. And men, who are often termed stupid, are not as stupid as they are being made out to be.

Children who learn what they live and live what they learn are also arguing and fighting with their parents. The home has become a verbal and physical battleground, with no fear or respect for each other anymore.

Their throat is an open tomb; With their tongues they have practiced deceit, the poison of asps is under their lips, whose mouth is full of cursing and bitterness. Their feet are swift to shed blood; Destruction and misery are in their ways; And the way of peace they have not known. There is no fear of God before their eyes. 46.

But if you are having a difficult time in your marriage, the last thing you should be doing is walking away. Adding to the more than one in three marriages that end in divorce is not the answer. The chances are that you will live to regret it, as outlined earlier. And the 'open tomb' that was dug by you and/or your partner may become your grave.

However, if you are put out of the family home for good, men, stay away from relationships in the short term. Sort yourselves out. The fact that you were kicked out won't hurt as much in the long run than if you walked away from your responsibilities. Your family then will almost certainly forget about you for good, and that is very likely to destroy you, which will be far more than you bargained for.

So if you have been kicked out, learn more about yourself and how to do things better next time; learn more also about females, especially modern women; read your bible for wisdom and understanding; then rebuild your finances to a much more powerful state. That is one of your strongest points—enterprise. Be in a much stronger position next time, so that no one takes liberties with you in future.

Spend a lot of quiet time with yourself in patience. Then the Lord will reveal a lot to you and how best to proceed, henceforth. No effort is needed—just patience and self-control, as you look to the long term. A lot more is achieved using patience and self-control than hurry and haste, which will make more waste, of an already wasteful life. You need to learn all over again the true meaning of life and how best to live.

Also, when the time comes to find a new partner, patience pays far better than haste. Put yourself back in control. Rediscover your masculine qualities, and one of them is that you are meant to lead not follow the fashion of the day, as they all come and go. But sound principles remain forever.

For one, the tranquillity and peace of mind that you will eventually gain from much time out spent to recharge all areas of your life, are indescribable and refreshing. And with new avenues opening themselves up to you, which started with those quiet moments spent with yourself, your happiness will return too.

If you focus on a problem it will become a gigantic thing. If you forget the problem, it perishes and becomes a futile thing. Then you can focus on what your true role in life is, using wisdom and understanding, which can only be gained from Christ the risen King. Most of us strive against our Lord and Saviour and become a gigantic failure. So instead of striving to find the right person, why not strive to become the right person with the risen King, who will turn your life around from sin, which He confines to the waste bin and give you a new and refreshing thing.

That is provided you do not put your foot back into another relationship in the immediate future, nor a one-night stand with anyone. Because these will bring fresh problems you don't need right now: problems, which will sink you much further in the murky spring and polluted well. 110.

One of your weaknesses is sex, and women know it. So they often use it as a tool in their armoury to beat you with and defeat you ultimately. Overcome as much as possible your need for sex, especially in a crisis. Little by little, *get over* your need for sex until the right time, instead of living *under it*, as it will crush you under its weight and destroy you. Do not give your strength to women, nor your ways to that which destroy kings. 47.

Once you rebuild yourself, which might take a few years, you will start seeing the benefits, which you should not allow anyone to take from you, henceforth. In those quiet times, you will find wisdom and renewed strength, instead of the unhealthy, wishy-washy, and clumsy circumstances you had found yourself in, when feminism ran riot in your life.

Compare that to the countless problems your previous wife or partner now has, as a single parent, bringing up probably several troubled children—trouble brought on by her decision to kick you out and selfishly denying the children their right to a father.

But do what you can to make matters bearable for the children, by keeping in contact with them, if you are allowed to, and supporting them financially and otherwise. Winston Churchill, probably Britain's greatest prime minister said, 'We make a living by what we get, but we make a life by what we give.' So seek to get and you will always be in debt and live by fret, but give and you will begin to live. Otherwise, that long sought-after peace and happiness will elude you in the same way it is eluding your ex.

In most circumstances, no matter what some may say, mothers are not able to inspire boys to great heights in the way that fathers can and often do. Many boys tend to rebel when there is only one parent in their lives. Children, especially boys, need fathers as well as mothers.

Some More Answers

*W*e know that it is not easy being and staying positive when those around you keep putting you down and are being negative, generally, about you. So who are those most likely to be openly negative about you?

If you are about to get into a relationship, learn this—the people who say the meanest things about us and do the meanest things to us are those we least expect it from. They are not our employers, our co-workers, or even our friends; they are our spouses and our family—the ones we hold dearest and nearest. Now brother will deliver up brother to death, and a father his child; and children will rise up against parents and cause them to be put to death, and a man's enemies will be those of his own household. 48.

Why should the worst in our personalities come from our nearest and dearest? The clues are in Matthew 10: 35, "For I have come to set a man against his father, a daughter against her mother, and a daughter-in-law against her mother-in-law." The Lord has revealed to me that the reason for this policy is for one member of the family, at least, to get the picture of not resting in the comfort of marital solidity, but to be aroused from his nest of rest and go and seek God's best.

Following on from this we know that familiarity breeds contempt. And the ones who are most familiar with us are our spouses. So if you are planning on making them change their ways toward you, you too will have to make some changes using **God's messages**, which will show your partner that you would like your relationship to survive the storm that it's currently going through.

There is more than a small chance that they will change their ways toward you. But for that to happen, it requires that you do not put the onus on the other party only, but put the onus of change firstly on yourself, and the rest will follow. This is very difficult to do, so you will have to work very hard at it, initially. But once in the flow you can begin to let go.

Initially it requires control, more control, and even more control—control your tongue, control your temper, and control your timing. Acting hastily only brings one bad decision after another. Acting hastily is not natural, as you then start to force issues. And anything forced tends to break before long, often with disastrous consequences.

Allow things to settle and be patient. In the quiet moments that you must find for yourself, God will reveal things to you—on what has been happening to you and how you should proceed, henceforth. No other effort is required but be patient and still and know that the Lord is God. Then wisdom, knowledge and understanding will flow in the stillness of the night or early morning, say. As a result, more will be achieved by you, using as few words as possible, and a few sensible decisions taken that will stand the test of time, earning you satisfaction and happiness in the end.

The fear of the Lord is the beginning of wisdom, And the knowledge of the Holy One is understanding. 49. In addition to His second coming, this is another reason why the Lord says, "watch", and not be taken in by sleep, so that you gain wisdom and understanding.

This will be in stark contrast to your normal pattern of several reckless words and decisions, as you leap from one crisis to another, possibly trying to correct the one before and the one before that and so on and so forth, thus rendering your life a complete ruin. In addition, you will live to regret it for a very long time—time which could be spent more wisely and in better ways.

In the meantime, what you have to do is put up and shut up, if you hope to make the breakthrough that you are looking for. Yes, I said put up and shut up. The alternatives, which are attractive, may appear easy, but they will only lead to more heartache, more pain, and more suffering. Quick fixes do not work. Haste makes waste. The long road leads to life, but short cuts lead to death.

A fool has no delight in understanding, but in expressing his own heart. 50.

Pride goes before destruction, and a haughty spirit before a fall 51.

A soft answer turns away wrath, but harsh words stir up anger. 52.

He who is slow to anger is better than the mighty, and he who rules his spirit than he who takes a city. 53.

Enter by the narrow gate, for wide is the gate and broad is the way that leads to destruction, and there are many who go in by it. Because narrow is the gate and difficult is the way which leads to life, and there are few who find it. 54.

If you are part of a family, married or not, and walk away from the situation you find yourself in, believe it or not, that will only make the situation worse. If you think about it, happiness and a contented lifestyle is not the destination you want to reach; it is the journey you are making each day, each hour, each minute to your various destinations. So don't opt out of any part of life's journey in the hope that happiness will then be a certainty. Don't settle for 'B' when glory is a distinct possibility.

When you opt out of parts of life's journey, you break the chain of possibilities to glory and stability. So you spend your time instead, turning back and looking back trying to fix your son Jack, and trying to avoid being nagged by your ex whom you call a slag.

Harvey Mackay tells the story of a professor who stood before his class of 30 final year molecular biology students.

Before passing out the final examination paper he said, 'I have been privileged to be your instructor this term, and I know how hard you have worked to prepare for this test. I also know most of you are off to medical school or post graduate study next autumn. I am well aware of how much pressure you are under to keep your grade point averages up. Because I am confident that you know this material, **I am prepared to offer an automatic B to anyone who opts to skip taking the final exam.**'

The relief was audible. A number of students jumped up from their desks, thanking the professor for the lifeline that he had thrown them.

'Any other takers?' he asked. 'This is your last opportunity.' One more student decided to go.

The instructor then handed out the final examination, which consisted of two sentences. It read: '**Congratulations, you have just received an A in this class. Keep believing in yourself.**' It was a just reward for the students who had worked hard and believed in themselves. Another lesson here is that most of us will jump to the call of anyone who will offer us what appears to be easy and quick fixes.

But the students given a B will be held in bondage and sadness by their consciences of how they cheated themselves out of the best. While those who received an A will have a free conscience and happiness, knowing that they settled for nothing less than their best. Responsibility is a two-sided coin. On one side is responsibility, on the other side is rewards. Too many of us are focused on one side of the coin only—rewards. Taking responsibility means three things:

1. Acknowledging what you are responsible for.
2. Acknowledging who you are responsible to.
3. Acting responsibly at all times.

All the excuses you give yourself, and others, won't let you off the hook. Jesus said, 'Much is required from those to whom much is given.' The apostle Paul experienced more headaches and heartaches in a month than most us will see in a lifetime. Yet he wrote, 'I can do all things through Christ who strengthens me.' 111. (**Source: UCB's The Word for Today**).

The few students who held on to the principles that life had taught them thus far, did not just get a visible A. They received the three A's of responsibility mentioned earlier, which are often not seen by others. While those who received a B showed no responsibility, but decided to ditch at a moment's notice the principles they had developed from the cradle till the moment they opted for the examination to be stopped.

So never give in to second best, or what under New Labour was called **dumbing down. Go for glory and tell your story.**

If you don't try to live a life of happy journeys, your destinations will be like hell's fury. Think about it. So why not make an effort at smiling when at times you feel like fighting and crying. Why not make an effort to stay the course when you feel like going for a divorce. Then things will be better when you have come to the end of your tether.

So if you are hoping or working on being happy and contented one day, you can forget it. It will never happen. You have to work to make each day, each hour and each minute of your life happy ones. So work on making happy those you get along with the least, and you, in turn, will be happier than when you started out. That is where you will achieve your greatest feat.

So don't opt for defeat by making them miserable or allowing them to get you upset. That will only make you unhappier than you were at the outset. You may think you have at last found happiness when you find someone new or when you go and live on your own. But that only brings new and unexpected troubles of their own; in addition to the baggage you carried forward, because you never dealt with them properly in the first place.

You chose to run away from your problems in the hope that you will have rid yourself of them finally. You do this by putting all the blame for your troubles on your previous partner.

By putting all the blame on your previous partner, you fail to see your own faults, and so you carry the same problems into your new relationship. If you listen carefully to yourself, you will hear a familiar tone to your voice whenever there is an argument between you and your new partner. The same suspicions that you had in the previous relationship are also thrown on to your new partner. All your previous insecurities come to the fore once you get familiar with your new partner, and things start going downhill again. So much for the old problems being carried forward.

What about the new problems you unintentionally pick up by your decisions made in anger and in haste, such as your decision to leave the family's place? In addition, there are more unwelcome problems emanating from other 'escape' routes such as drink, drugs, gambling and sampling materials and substances not suitable for anyone, let alone someone suffering from the psychological and physical problems brought on by being sidelined by his once loving spouse.

The man who has no inner life is a slave to his surroundings. He falls prey to sin and becomes a part of hell's waste bin. This bin chains, shocks and stifles. A man of inner life and spirit is free of his surroundings, as he is guided from above to live above. So prepare to climb out of that waste bin.

Because, as Henry Ford observed, 'before everything else, getting ready is the secret of success.'

The frustrating thing about preparation is that sometimes it takes more time than the actual event you're preparing for. There's an old saying: 'You can claim to be surprised once; after that you are unprepared.'

You'll never be successful if you're forever putting things off. If you take too long to make your mind up about an opportunity, you'll miss out on seizing it. Safe living generally makes for regrets later on.

We are all given talents and dreams. Sometimes the two don't seem to match. But usually we compromise both before ever finding out. Later on, we find ourselves looking back longingly to that time when we should have chased our true dreams and our true talents for all they are worth.

Don't let yourself be pressured into thinking that your dreams or talents aren't prudent. They were never meant to be prudent. They were meant to bring joy and fulfilment into your life.

If a caterpillar refuses to get into its cocoon it'll never transform and will be forever relegated to crawling on the ground, even though it had the potential to fly.

You cannot be like Alice in Through The Looking Glass, who asks the Cheshire cat: 'Would you please tell me which way I ought to go from here?'

'That depends on where you want to get,' the cat replies.

'I don't care much where,' she answers.

'Then it doesn't matter which way you go,' the cat responds.

That's living and accepting the life of a 'bum', thinking that it will all end in fun.

People who are undecided cannot draw on their faith and their gifting.

What do you believe God called you to do? Do it! God's not limited by your IQ, He is limited by your, 'I will'.

The poet said, 'If you think you are beaten, you are. If you think you dare not, you don't. If you'd like to win but think you can't, it's almost certain that you won't. Life's battles don't always go to the stronger or faster man, but sooner or later the man who wins, is the man who believes he can. (**Source: UCB's Word for Today**).

One of the consequences of your decision to opt for defeat, would be that your children will start to experience difficulties in life that they did not ask for. One or more of them might start rebelling against the dictates of one or both parents resulting directly from the break-up of their parents' relationship.

This may result in one of them starting to look to their friends, possibly a gang, for acceptance and guidance in the absence of a parent who seemingly rejected them.

There are 'destiny moments' when you have to make life-changing choices. One day Jesus invited two people to join His team, but they both had their reasons for putting it off. One had a funeral to attend, the other wanted to go home to explain his decision. That's the last we hear of them. Matthew records, '... He got into a boat, His disciples followed Him.' 112. They missed the boat!

If you take too long to make your mind up about an opportunity, you'll miss out on seizing it.

One of the best illustrations of this is the story about the patent of the telephone. In the 1870's two men worked extensively on modifying and improving telegraphy, which was the current technology. Both had ideas of transmitting sound by wire, and both explored the transmission of human voice electronically.

What is remarkable is that both men, Alexander Graham Bell and Elisha Gray, filed their idea at the patent office on the same day—February 14, 1876. Bell was the fifth person that day to file for a patent.

Gray, on the other hand, got busy with other things, so he sent his attorney. Unfortunately, the attorney arrived more than half an hour after Bell, to apply for a caveat, a kind of declaration of intention to file for a patent. Obviously, Gray did not pay due diligence to this important matter and so suffered the consequences.

Those minutes cost Gray a fortune. Bell's claim was upheld in court, even though Gray complained that he had come up with the idea first. So it is not enough to see your God-given opportunities, you have to seize them. In other words don't miss the boat! (Source: UCB's The Word for Today).

So happiness does not come by getting away or running away from your troubles and opting for 'safe' living. It comes from getting to know who you truly are, who your spouse truly is, who Christ is; and therefore, how to deal with your troubles by making the best use of the opportunities that present themselves. And that is what I am about to set out in the next chapters: being happy despite what people think or say about you.

Living a Life of Lies

People will always point the finger. Very rarely will someone say 'I was wrong, and I am very sorry for what I have done.' When we point the index finger at someone, usually in an accusing gesture, all the other fingers are pointing back at ourselves. We don't see the fingers pointing back at ourselves, but we see the one pointing at others. Have you ever thought about that?

Similarly, we very rarely see our own faults, but are always quick to see the faults of others and expose them, even in front of others without a thought for that person's feelings. How would we like it done to us? No, that's not a problem, because we are never at fault. That's the attitude we adopt.

People do not like to confront their own faults. As far as most people are concerned, we have few faults worth talking about, while others we know have more faults than we have time to talk about. So we live in denial. Very few of us recognise our own faults and would like to do something about them. The vast majority blames others for their problems, and these are usually the most vocal of people.

Wise people store up knowledge, but the mouth of the foolish is near destruction. 55.

He who guards his mouth preserves his life, but he who opens wide his lips shall have destruction. 56. The way of a fool is right in his own eyes, but he who heeds counsel is wise. 57.

There is one who speaks like the piercings of a sword, but the tongue of the wise promotes health. 58. A wholesome tongue is a tree of life, but perverseness in it breaks the spirit. 59. A fool has no delight in understanding, but in expressing his own heart. 60.

But whether we recognise our faults or not, nearly all of us are afraid to confront ourselves, own up to what we have done wrong, and do something about them. It is easy to do the act, but when it comes to facing facts and their consequences, we become frightened of doing the right thing.

The reasons we do not like to face the consequences of our actions and do the right thing are manifold. One is, doing the right thing will cost us; it may cost us our jobs; it may cost us a relationship, such as a marriage; it may cost us a lot of money; it may land us in prison; or we may be let off with only a stern talking-to for telling the truth in the first place.

We focus keenly on one side of the coin and not on the fact that we may be let off.

Confess your trespasses to one another and pray for one another, that you may be healed. 61. Yes, if you confess you will redress the wrongs between you and yours, and you will have purged yourself of that terrible curse, forgiven and made new again oh ladies and gentlemen.

But we fail to look at the other side of the coin, which telling lies and hiding facts will bring. We may still lose our jobs or lose a relationship such as a marriage; it may cost us a lot of money; and it may land us in prison with the certainty of an even longer term than if we had told the truth in the first place.

We may get away with it, but the prospect of carrying the burden of hidden facts and lies, and the thought of the people we have hurt for the rest of our lives is not something easy to live with. So instead of being free from our actions and their consequences, we carry hidden burdens for the rest our lives.

Some of us have to do so much to continue keeping the facts of our actions from others by continually lying, in order to try and get away with it. Others have to go into hiding, protected sometimes by armed thugs to keep justice at bay, while others still, find it necessary to mask their features by wearing a beard and/or glasses to try and keep their true identity a secret. So we move from telling lies and doing evil deeds to living a life of lies and deception in order to return to some semblance of normality and freedom, which we once had.

So while we may get away with the actions we have indulged in for a while, in the meantime we have to face our own consciences, which keep us in our internal prison and keep us from being truly free. Every day our consciences will remind us over and over again about the things that we have done to others and consequently to ourselves.

We may choose to be silent or lie before a court of law or to our families and friends, but we cannot lie to our consciences, which will keep us in prison for the rest our lives or until we come clean before the people we have hurt, and before God.

Not only can one not lie to one's conscience, and to God, but it will also make one miserable, keep one prisoner in one's own mind, suffocate and may even kill one with the burden one has fostered on it; or make one so ill, one can't even keep still, but is tormented till one's mind is fomented, making one worse still.

In addition, we have the additional difficulty of keeping up appearances in front of all those we meet, pretending to be someone or something we are not. No one can keep telling or living a lie forever. For some people, it is several lies. We are certain to be found out. Then we will be knocked out for the count when all is spilt and sprout. Our own actions will trip us up at some point. And the consequences will be far worse then than if we had faced up to our actions far earlier. Who would want to live like that?

The wicked is banished in his wickedness, But the righteous has a refuge in his death. 62.

Evil pursues sinners, But to the righteous good shall be repaid. 63. A true witness delivers souls, But a deceitful witness speaks lies. Good understanding gains favour, but the way of the unfaithful is hard. 64. The merciful man does good for his own soul, But he who is cruel troubles his own flesh. 65. The integrity of the upright will guide them, but the perversity of the unfaithful will destroy them. 66. The way of the wicked is like darkness; *they do not know what makes them stumble.* 67. Pride goes before destruction, And a haughty spirit before a fall. 68. A false witness shall not go unpunished, And he who speak lies shall perish. 69.

Though there are consequences for doing the right thing, the earlier it is done, the better it is for the perpetrator in the long run. Those consequences are more likely to be short-term because we have done the right thing in the end and before it is too late. We will have saved ourselves so much pain, heartaches, illnesses, and even early death.

Do you have a prodigal heart? The parable of the prodigal son teaches us that by listening to God we can avoid tragedy; that by living under His rule we are saved from our misguided tendencies. Jesus said, 'There was a man who had two sons. The younger one said ... "Father, give me my share" ... Not long after ... (he) ... set off for a distant country and there he squandered his wealth in wild living. After he had spent everything, there was a severe famine ... and he began to be in need. So he went and hired himself out ... to feed pigs. He longed to fill his stomach with the pods that the pigs were eating, but no one gave him anything.' 125. When God says no, heed Him. When He pulls back on the reins, thank Him.

It's better to be alone and walk with God, than be surrounded by those who'll hurt you. Prodigal, things won't improve until you start doing things God's way! Are you willing to repent and come back home? In three back-to-back parables, in Luke 15, Jesus pointed out that the shepherd went looking for his lost sheep, the woman went looking for her lost silver, but nobody went looking for the lost son. That's because he knew the way back. And it happened **when 'he came to his senses.'**

The rebel who left home saying, **'Give me'**, humbled himself and came back saying, **'Forgive me'.** When he did, his father embraced him and said, 'This son of mine was . . . lost and is found . . .' 126. **Today your heavenly Father is waiting to welcome you home. (Source: UCB's The Word for Today).**

The consequences, as I have mentioned, of doing the right thing is far more short-termed than if the problem is left to fester. We all know about the sores that are left untreated. Well, it is the same thing for human relations.

Doing the right thing means humbling ourselves: it means coming down from our high horse or the tree on which you have perched ourselves and eating humble pie, which is facing up to what we have done. It means accepting the help to get down from such high places so that our fall from grace will be cushioned, instead of having a fall that will shatter our lives in more ways than we could have imagined. It means being humiliated in front of our families or whomever it is that we have offended. It means facing up to our feelings being hurt, because we are ashamed of what we have done to others.

So if your once happy home has been rocked by infidelity, come clean to your partner as soon as possible to avoid a lifetime of imprisoned pain. In the short term you will have cast your burdens on your partner's shoulder, but fortunately, in the long term, you will have begun the healing process.

In the long term, it means that you will benefit from a free conscience for doing the right thing. This feeling of freedom that you carry for the rest of your life, instead of a lifetime burden of lies and hidden facts, is indescribable.

But in the short term, your partner will be hurting. They will bring up your infidelity time and time again as the pain reveals itself inside out. They will use it to tear you to threads because they are truly hurting. Just imagine someone who has had a serious burn to the flesh. They constantly scream in anguish. Well, it is the same thing. The only difference is that the pain is on the inside.

After a while you may not be thinking about the hurt they are going through. You will think about the hurt that is now happening to you. You will be saying, 'What more does she want me to do? I have apologised over and over again.' So forgiveness seems to take forever, or it does not seem to be happening at all.

Forgiveness is happening; it's just not happening on your watch. The fact that she has not thrown you out is a sign that the process has begun. Learn to listen more and talk less. Give your partner space instead of adding fuel to the fire by constantly being in her face. Learn to be more understanding and be more patient.

If you are truly contrite, the process of forgiveness will be a lot shorter. Go out of your way to rebuild the relationship, instead of being angry and frustrated at every angry out burst from her. Imagine what the reaction would be if you were to be found out instead of you coming forward and owning up to what you have done. Surely it would be far worse, and we all know it. You would very likely lose everything you worked so many years to achieve.

But still, when in a serious situation, most of us choose to tell lies or hide the truth.

We don't want to hurt our feelings or want anyone to hurt us, so we lash out in an act of self-preservation and self-defence, casting the blame for our problems and our failings on someone else and on our loved ones especially. We adopt the motto that attack is the best form defence. Where a still tongue is required to allow the fire to burn itself out, we, instead, pour more fuel on the fire, winding up the other party further as a way of getting out of the situation we find ourselves in.

On the one hand, we may be bottling up something inside, such as an affair or a passionate kiss, hoping that no one will find out. On the other hand, we may want to come clean to free ourselves from the bondage that we find ourselves in.

However, holding on to something like this and not releasing it to those who matter only make us unhappy, irritable, unstable, insecure, and on the edge all the times. It makes us unstable, because whereas coming clean often makes us put the past behind us, holding on to it causes us to seek solace and comfort in repeating the same mistake over and over again until things get truly out of hand.

Then our partner, or whoever needs to know, will find out one way or the other, as the longer you continue in the same vein, the easier it becomes for someone to find out or for you to get caught. Also the longer we continue, the more obvious it becomes from our activities that something is not quite right. In addition, our facial features will soon reveal that we have been living a lie when questioned, or suspicion arises in some form.

It makes us unhappy, because after the high of the deceit, which lasts a short time, the low sets in and lasts far longer and lasts until it is dealt with properly. And refusing to deal with it or having a fear of dealing with the deceit will only prolong our misery and make the problems deep-rooted, eventually.

We may pretend to be happy in front of our families or friends, but our edginess will eventually start showing in the form of irritability and sudden bursts of anger.

It can also make us insecure, as we often get paranoid about our spouses' behaviour. We ask such questions as, 'What is she doing behind my back?' Because we are insecure ourselves and are not at peace with ourselves, because of our own actions when no one else is looking, we think that our spouse must be doing the same thing. This breeds more and more insecurity and untrustworthiness in relationships, often leading to fights and even separation.

And paranoia can become such a big problem that it can lead to a full-blown psychotic illness of destructive proportions—and all because we could not trust ourselves in the first place.

So living a lie is never worth it. It opens a Pandora's box that you will not be able to control, unless you come clean and make a 'u' turn. So to prevent these problems from festering, come clean as soon as possible. Put yourself and your partner out of their misery. As the saying goes, 'Speak the truth and the truth will make you free.'

This saying is so true, because although you experience the downside of humiliation when you 'spill the beans', when the dust is settled, you will experience the lift like a hot air balloon heading upwards—the lift of a big burden being removed from your heart and shoulders.

Release your thoughts and experience the lift you need. No one is perfect; we all make mistakes. It is what we do with those mistakes and lessons we learn or fail to learn that makes the difference between better or worse for us.

Go on, release your burdens on someone else's shoulders, and give yourself a break. Confide in someone if you find it difficult to talk to your spouse, but release it. We are not designed to carry secretive burdens. They can cause ill health and eventually kill us. So why hang on to something that can potentially make us unwell? In addition, you will nearly always be grumpy as a result of your burdens, which are proving too much for you to live joyfully.

Your spouse may or may not initially forgive you for what you have done to yourself and your family. But whatever he or she comes back to you with, it is far better than you holding on to something that could eventually cause greater harm to you and your family.

History shows that once you tell the truth, initially you may not be forgiven for it. Whenever there is a conflict between you and your spouse, he or she will invariably remind you of your weaknesses and your failures.

You could hear words like, 'You are a no-good, cheating scumbag. Why don't you get lost and never be found? I hate you. You have hurt me and the kids so much. You should be ashamed of what you have done to us. You don't deserve this family. You have forfeited your right to be a part of this family!'

How do you respond to rage like that? The truth is you don't respond. Allow your spouse to blow off steam, because you adding your tongue to the situation will only make things worse. And in some cases, that is what your spouse wants. He or she wants you to attack with words of your own so you can feel the full force of their anger.

Anger indeed kills the fool. Anger will destroy you and not the person you are attacking. The person attacking is slowly being destroyed by his or her own anger. Soft words turn away wrath.

So if you feel forced to respond to your spouse's onslaught, use words of understanding, though their words may be cutting you like a knife. But the best way to avoid being badly hurt is to walk away and live to fight on another day.

Standing there, engaging in a mouth-to-mouth combat is like pouring fuel into the flames and stoking the fire. This can lead to the situation getting out of hand. And when the situation gets out of hand, who knows what the end result will be? Whatever it turns out to be, it will certainly not be something you planned for or wanted. It will be something you live to regret. That is what I meant by Pandora's box that you wouldn't be able to control.

Walking away from a situation is a decision you make and which you have more control over. This is like turning the fire off or allowing the flame to burn itself out. In this situation, your spouse no longer has anyone to vent his or her anger on, so he or she either stops or argue with his or herself. Over time, he or she will become less and less interested in arguing to win a point, as he or she knows that there will be no one to argue with.

Of all the options, this clearly is the best one. Counselling can help, but no amount of counselling will necessarily solve the problem of arguing. If a person is inclined to argue their point, they will continue to do it despite what was agreed in the counselling. In the heat of the moment, rationality goes out the window.

You won't necessarily change people by counselling, and arguing certainly will not help. People are people, and we get more entrenched in our ways the older we get or when someone appears to be humiliating us. The best method for success is to allow God to heal. Little by little, you will start to forgive each other. We have all heard the saying that 'Time is the greatest healer'. Well, it is God that does the healing and it is very true. In the meantime, you have got some putting up and shutting up to do. These changes in you are what will cause them to follow suit, too: When a man's ways please the Lord, He makes even his enemies to be at peace with him. 141.

Learning to resist reacting to provocation is one of the first lessons anyone in a relationship needs to learn in the journey of allowing God to heal. If you are going to allow God to heal your relationship, you have to avoid joining in the war of words, as this will only delay the point at which your relationship gets healed.

Difficult though it is to stay calm and hold your peace under pressure, stay calm and hold your peace under pressure you must. Once again, the alternative is far worse. Take a break by walking away from the situation if you must, but sink to his or her level by joining in you must not. He who guards his mouth preserves his life, but he who opens wide his lips shall have destruction. 70.

If you are a man, you are not likely to win a war of words anyhow, as from the outset you are in a verbal mismatch. Women are, among other things, built to argue their point, while men are not built to argue their point with a woman to the same extent.

So it is easy to lose your cool when someone gets under your skin with the words they use to break in. That point of being broken down verbally is very dangerous, as your feelings are so injured that you could do something irrational. But lose your cool you must not, because the consequences far outweigh and outlive the initial action. So before you jump in to hit her look at the bigger picture.

Say for instance, you put your hand on your partner, they are likely to strike you back, causing you serious injury, which may require hospitalisation. Or worse still, that person could wait till you are asleep to do you serious harm—harm he or she would be wary of doing while you were awake. Equally bad, that person could put something poisonous in your food, which happens.

But the more likely scenario is that that person could call the police. Now if you are a man complaining about your wife's assault, you are not likely to call the police for several reasons: One reason is that because you are a man, you should be able to cope with it and bear it; another reason is that you love your wife and do not want to cause you and your family any more harm than has already been done. Another, still, is that men are sometimes more forgiving than their partners, so you will sit and take the blows, whatever the consequences, in the hope that one day she will change her ways for better days.

But another reason you are not likely to call the police, which no one talks about these days, is because assaults by wives on their husbands are not taken seriously at all by the authorities. Domestic violence by women on men is increasing dramatically, given women's newly found lease of power in today's society. But very few women have resultantly been arrested, unless the assault is very serious or of a life-threatening nature.

In our society, whereby in the home women have become more equal than men, it is not the thing to do—to arrest a female spouse—nor is it spoken about seriously. It is a taboo subject. So in such circumstances where men are assaulted by their wives, he is more likely to be arrested instead, if a complaint has been made.

However, for a man assaulting his wife, the consequences are far more serious. She is far more likely to call the police. Then you will be arrested. There are no ifs or buts as it is, if it is the other way around. You will be put into a cell; your DNA will be taken for the police national computer database.

You will be interviewed under caution. Then the crown prosecution service will make the final decision on whether you are to be charged, be cautioned, or no further action is to be taken. Usually, your wife won't take any further action anyhow. This will have a bearing on what the CPS decides to do in the end. But the final decision lies in their hands.

Compare that robust set of actions, to the mostly non-existent policy to assaults by wives on the main person in their lives.

Although she may not want you to have criminal record, she could take additional action, banning you from coming anywhere near the family home for a period of time. As a man, the odds are not stacked in your favour, so think before you act and keep your life intact. If you are not in a position to think straight, walk straight away and give yourself time and space to think clearly, otherwise you will pay dearly.

Spend that time and use that space to learn more about your spouse and yourself from the situation you find yourself in, so that you do not make similar mistakes for future's sake. Christ said come to Me all you who labour and are heavily laden, and I will give you rest. For My yoke is easy and My burden is light. 71. The law of the wise is a fountain of life, to turn one away from the snares of death. 72. Good understanding gains favour, . . . 73. And, . . . through knowledge the righteous will be delivered. 74.

Working at Life

*N*othing in life is meant to be easy. We are meant to work at life to build our characters, to become eventually the successes we are meant to be as indicated in the parable of the talents in Matthew's gospel. We are given talents and we are meant to build and increase on what we were given, not finding escape routes of living, but building solid foundations that stand the test of time whatever is thrown at them.

One observation about us men, is that it appears that we are not built to be monogamous, while for women, the opposite appears to be the truth. But what is undeniable is that we are made to live in monogamous relationships, because anything other than a monogamous relationship only brings disaster and resulting unhappiness for all concerned.

Therefore, we are made to work at our relationships so that they stand the test of time. It is important that our relationships stand the test of time because that is the only way to achieve true and long-lasting happiness and the resulting stability we all crave for.

There are so many possibilities for happiness and success when our families work on their weaknesses and failures to achieve the best for one another. *Such possibilities are significantly reduced when we are divided and our relationships end up in separation rendering a generation to annihilation.*

Each of us draws his or her strength from the family when it is a unit. We see the possibilities of success, and our hopes and dreams are boundless.

Children, especially those brought up in a successful marriage, do not usually drop out of school or end up in a life of crime. Instead, they end up as graduates from university and go on to successful careers. Therefore, they become a net contributor to society and are not a drain on the public purse, which many single-parent families become.

Their children also follow their parents' example and get married themselves, viewing this learnt way of life as the best method of bringing up and rearing a successful family. These facts are undeniable as surveys after surveys have borne this out, and the Bible, which always come to past, have said as much. When you joined the ranks of modern women, This is the rejoicing city that dwelt securely, that said in her heart, "I am it, and there is none besides me." How has she become a desolation . . . . But the unjust knows no shame. Zephaniah 2:15; 3:5. For where envy and self-seeking exist, confusion and every evil thing are there. James 3:16. God's way is always the best way. . . . what God has joined together, let not man separate, . . . Matthew 19:6. In addition, generations in the past, when marriages were more common compared to today, were more successful in rearing families . . . . It is not good that man should be alone; I will make him a helper comparable to him. 75. Therefore a man shall leave his father and mother and be joined to his wife, and they shall become one flesh. 76.

Take away the man from the family-fold, and you begin to see the break up of families and the broken society we see today. Men living on their own do not fare well, as the Bible says. And women living as single parents have proven to be bad for children especially. This is not the way things were meant to be.

Sadly, this is the common state of affairs in Britain today, brought about largely as a result of government policies, directly and indirectly, which discourage marriage and promote single parenthood through the tax and benefit system and the number of agencies set up to benefit women only. Through the government's hostility to marriage, mediocrity is now being promoted as the way forward over success, and successful people are being made to feel guilty for the failures of the unsuccessful.

A recent UN survey shows that Britain is now the worst place in the developed world for children to grow up. For many, there is little or no surprise at this, given government policies over the past decade or so.

So life has been made so much more difficult for us fathers over the past decade. Therefore, it is equally important that although our wives and partners are given a leg-up and immense powers, whereby they are now more equal than their husbands in the home, we should fight for our families when faced with eviction.

Not only should we fight for our families for our sakes, but also for the sake of our children, who will be the biggest losers, as well as for society's sake.

Take away the father from the family and some of our children, especially boys, lose all sense of direction and identity. Their lives and future have just been taken away from them, through acts of selfishness. And when that happens, many look to their peers for direction, and that direction could be a life of crime and grime.

Another possible law that will not only make the husband and father's life more difficult, but could also easily cost him his life, is the rule that says a woman can kill him, if she fears being attacked at some point in the future.

In the home men were less than valuable, but now it's implied that their lives are no longer valued either, because his wife can kill him and get away with a mere manslaughter charge or get off completely.

What goes around comes around, and centuries of oppression of women by men have been turned around against today's men. Now a lot of men will be wary before getting seriously involved with women in today's climate.

Where in the past, a woman would think twice about killing her husband, if this law is introduced, she won't necessarily have to, because the chances are that she will get away with it, without even a custodial sentence.

So if a woman loathes her husband and his very existence, all she has to do is kill him, make up a story backed by a clever lawyer, get away with it as most of them do anyhow with the law as it stands, and start a new life with the possibility of doing the same thing to her new man if he is not careful.

Twenty-first Century Reality

$\mathcal{T}$he twenty-first century will be very significant for families as the top-down changes fostered on it will be so profound that it will not be able to cope. It will be pulled apart by left-wing forces, and right-wing forces will apply a patchwork effect. But the damage done by the left will be so deep-seated that we will continue to see the demise of the traditional family and its awful consequences for a very long time to come. Government policies aimed at uplifting women at the expense of men will see to that. As divorce and separation cases rise, men will start to wonder what has hit them, as they get hurled out of their families one by one.

The financial effect on the social services, police, prisons, hospitals, and courts will negate any economic growth made, and it will make economic growth more difficult too.

It already makes more financial sense for women to live on their own than to have someone move in with them. The benefit system pays them more if they live on their own than if they live with a partner. So there is no incentive to start and build a family. The government plunges families into disaster by the effect of their policies, but they have no interest in correction by re-encouraging families to stay together.

Instead, their answer is to put Antisocial Behaviour Orders on youngsters when their lives inevitably go wrong, and many take this as a badge of honour to behave antisocially. They make it easy for women to have abortions; make it easier and acceptable for women to have affairs, and make it easier for them to kill their husbands and partners. How are these measures going to make families better is beyond me. But probably they are not meant to do so.

These policies seem to be designed to destroy families and give women the 'freedom' many of them have so longed for.

But how is having an estranged partner on drink, drugs, in a mental hospital, in prison, homeless, or even dead meant to bring freedom to the other sex? That is increasingly the effect on men when they are forced out of the family home. Have we lost all compassion for each other as a society? What a sad state of affairs when this becomes the reality we live in today.

How is having children arguing and fighting with their mother, then leaving the home to seek guidance from their peers, who often lead them into a life of crime and grime, meant to bring freedom to the other sex?

How is making abortion easier and the emotional problems of regret that comes with it meant to bring freedom to the other sex?

What's meant to be freedom and choice is instead bringing more bondage, pain, and misery for women. You can't turn centuries of tradition and cohesion on its head and expect something fitter and better. You are bound to end up with a stinker that is a sinker of any ship let alone marriage and relationships.

Statistics still show, and will always show, that families where the children are brought up by two parents who are married are the happiest, the most stable, and the most successful. And when these families are Christians, this is even more the case. So why make haste to destroy the family base?

There is more freedom, choice, and ultimately happiness when we are together, when we are in bondage to each other. We build each other up when we work together for the good of one another. We feed off each other for our needs, instead of looking outside for a ride at the expense of wife or hussy who thinks everything is fine. For indeed you will suffer the runs if all you are looking for is a bit of fun.

Children learn what is right and good by following the example of their parents who are united and understood. They learn what is wrong and bad when rage is ignited and the parents are divided. Children are protected from the ills of society when their parents speak with a united voice to see that they stay in line and not fall to these evil times. They are also protected from society's evils and frivolity when their parents don't indulge in infidelity. So interdependence should be promoted, not the myth of independence.

When they see their parents bickering, fighting, and divided, they also learn to bicker, fight, and rebel against their parents and society, which leads to untold social and economic problems.

When the parents are united and lead moral lives, they are able to protect their children from the excesses of television, video games, and Internet, which are wreaking untold damage on the easily impressionable minds of our children.

Children live what they learn and learn what they live. When they are brought up in a united family where the parents are married, they tend to turn out to be well-rounded members of society, who make a net positive contribution to the development of the country. They live longer, happier, healthier lives, go on to get married, and bring up a family in a similar manner themselves.

When they are brought up by a single parent, usually the mother, their prospects in life are inevitably less rosy. Many women say they don't need a man and can do things all on their own, but the statistics tell a different story. One such statistic says that Britain is now the worst place in the developed world for children to grow up.

People go against nature and expect success. Thank God that things were not meant to be that way so that one day, somewhere down the line, we have to come face to face with ourselves and finally accept where we have gone wrong when things don't work out as we expected them to. We can't always blame someone else for our failures.

The Bible says that it is not good for a man to be alone, so God gave him a helper. Women are meant to help their husbands, not turn on them. We have turned the natural order of things into an unnatural situation and expect progress.

As a result, children, especially boys, will continue to lose direction, as sooner or later, there will be no fathers left to help direct them. Many people now say that children in Britain are the most rebellious in the world. In the inner cities especially, where family breakdown is at crisis proportions, children are rebelling against society like never before. In some areas the trend is to take over communities to the fear and trepidation of the law-abiding citizens. And it all started in the home, or more accurately put, from top-down policies of the government.

Despite economic progress over the past decade or so, children, in increasing numbers, are losing hope and faith in this society and their broken families. They have lost that innocence and respect for their elders and are now taking on their elders and society verbally and even physically. They have lost that respect also for authority that used to be entrenched in British society.

So, 'Direct your children onto the right path.' 142. When Harry and AdaMaeDay brought their first child Sandra home from the hospital, it was to a tiny ranch house without running water, electricity or a school within driving distance. But they refuse to let their surroundings limit them. His father's death had precluded Harry from attending Stanford University (one of America's top universities), but he never lost hope that his daughter would study there.

Ada Mae subscribed to educational newspapers and magazines, home-schooled her daughter and later sent her to the best boarding schools. Sandra did attend Stanford, the law school and eventually became the first woman Supreme Court Justice in America. The day she was sworn in she donned her robes and took her place among the other justices. Then she locked her eyes with her family and the tears began.

Don't buy into the modern mindset of feminism that devalues motherhood by putting careers first; there is no more important job on earth, apart from serving the Lord. Solomon said, 'Direct your children onto the right path, and when they are older, they will not leave it.' (**Source: UCB's The Word for Today**).

But these days many children don't know much better as they are confused when they see their mother and father fighting and them being abused, when they see their mother, for instance, behaving like a man, when she is getting stoned with drink and losing her dignity in the streets, when they offer their children a drink at an early age, or when they see their mother with different men in a short space of time.

Even the police are taking a beating in the streets from our children. Not only do many of them not respect their elders any more, they also have no fear of them nor the law. As a result, they now have no inhibitions. They do what they like, when they like, and wherever they like, without fear of being caught and punished. Children are now even willing to murder their peers, should they cross their paths, often using the most flippant of excuses or reasons for their actions.

In many communities, many children roam the streets even late at nights in gangs and mobs. Mob rule has now taken over many communities. The fear of authority and our elders has long gone out from the minds and hearts of our children.

That fear has now largely been transferred from children to parents, particularly single parents, communities, and authorities. The government has made it a crime to physically punish our children. So parents now fear laying a hand on their own children. An increasing number of children are now warning their parents that if they touch them, they are going to call the police. Increasing number of parents, too, are now being arrested for assaulting their children. In many parts of Britain, children are now out of control, as a result.

Children now know that they can get away with nearly anything and they know how far they can push their parents and society to. So without hesitation they push things to the limit and sometimes even beyond. They have become very manipulative, and some have claimed the streets in their communities for themselves, doing what they want, when they want.

Be warned. The rod and rebuke gives wisdom, but a child left to himself brings shame to his mother. 77. Correct your son and he will give you rest; yes, he will give delight to your soul. 78.

Men's ideas and philosophies come and go very quickly. People vote them in and people vote them out. But what the Bible teaches us has been relevant through all generations. Men have always gone against what the Bible teaches, hence they have always ended up with failure. So ignore the Bible at your peril.

The small enclaves of rural communities are some of the few places where one can find children's innocence and obedience to parents and authority still intact. However, aspects of inner city disorder are making inroads into rural communities too.

The Benefits of Avoiding Trivialities

One of the things that causes friction in the relationship of a husband and wife is when one party jumps to some conclusion. It is very easy to jump to a conclusion when you think that you have suffered wrongs by your partner. We fly off the handle before finding out the facts, when sometimes there could be an entirely innocent explanation for what appears to have gone wrong.

Say for instance, you have not been getting along very well with your wife and some of your clothes go missing; you assume that your wife has destroyed them because she has done it before. You immediately jump on the bandwagon with a barrage of tongue-lashing and accusations, which could easily lead to a nasty situation between you both. Although she denies it, you carry on. Then you look in the cupboard for something else one day and, lo and behold, your clothes turn up in the most unexpected of places. Suddenly your memory has been jogged, and you remember putting them there. Or your wife put them there without thinking or remembering.

So you realise that you have made a mistake by jumping to your own conclusions. The thing to do then is to humble yourself, apologise, make up and learn your lesson. But in most cases, pride takes precedence, and you don't even acknowledge that you have found the clothes, but carry on as if nothing has happened. This does not bode well for your relationship, as you are not learning from your mistakes. **Eventually your pride will cause you great harm and**

possibly destroy your relationship and you as a person. Every prudent man acts with knowledge, but a fool lays open his folly. 79. The discretion of a man makes him slow to anger, and his glory is to overlook a transgression. 80.

So the moral of the story is this: when you think that your spouse has done you wrong, hold your peace and wait, then wait, and wait again. Cut out all thinking until you have cooled down, because when you are worked up, your thoughts are more likely to lead to bad decisions.

Once you have cooled down, then you can start to think in a more rational manner on what might or might not have gone wrong. If you fail to come up with the answer, the answer will come to you when you least expect it, possibly by your very partner—the person you were about to accuse—and quite possibly, wrongfully. And often the answer is likely to be something entirely innocent and something you least expected. Then wisdom and understanding will come as a breath of fresh air when you have found your things.

Think of all the headaches, suffering, and regret you will have avoided by holding your peace and waiting for the answer to turn up from the most unlikely of sources and the least expected of places and get the most unexpected of explanations. Life is strange; life is a mystery. So don't hurry to get prickly until you can see where you are going, because you could fall into a pit, which would be a great pity.

You will have avoided, possibly, a major crisis over what may well be a minor triviality. Trivialities are often what cause the most stresses and strains in marriages. And so we can say from experience that most arguments between couples are entirely unnecessary.

The more you argue, the more she will argue back, and usually, she is more disposed to arguing than you are. This will only make you both more and more frustrated and unhappy. This way of living leads only in one direction, which is downwards, and ultimately, it will cause the destruction of your relationship and possibly both or one of you too.

The less you argue, the less she will argue too, leading to a more peaceful, relaxed, and happier environment. Soon you will be talking more than you arguing, leading to better understanding between you two and better tolerance of each other. This will, in turn, lead you to draw closer to each other, and your relationship will grow stronger as a result.

Then the benefits will be endless. Cooperation will increase between both of you, and you will do more things together. You will grow happier as a result, and the bond between you both will strengthen. Soon you will dislike arguing and will try to avoid it at all costs, because you will know from experience where it is likely to lead to and the likely costs.

Your new and refreshing relationship will rub off on your children too, who will engage with you and their siblings in like manner. They too will lead happier lives as a result, which means they are less likely to look elsewhere for happiness.

But it all starts with you holding your tongue and your peace for the greater good. It starts with you realising that you are not in this on your own. The family matters an awful lot and they should come first in all your actions, then selfishness will take more and more of a back seat.

Only by putting others before yourself will you find true and lasting happiness. At work, you put the customer first because if we don't, we lose them and ultimately, our jobs. But for some strange reason we fail to see that the same principle applies to our family.

We argue, fuss, and fight with our family, but we dare not do the same to our customers. We treat the customers nicely and make sure that they are satisfied, but we don't do the same with our family.

So to show that you care more than they think you do, how about surprising them from time to time by buying, for example, something your wife always wanted or something you know she likes or needs badly, but which she does not expect you to buy.

It shows that you have them in mind even when you are physically far apart.

Role Reversal

oday men have a very different role in the home than the role they had even ten years ago. Men no longer seem certain what their role is any more. As women go out to work in increasing numbers under changes influenced by the feminist movement, men appear to have lost their way and are confused, as they find themselves doing more and more of the household chores.

It's a completely unnatural state of affairs. So although most men are willing to take on more and more of the household chores, they often struggle to break into this new frontier.

As the wife finds less time for the home, the man helps out in the house for many reasons: One is to please his wife, so that she is more likely to make love with him. But this often does not work, because, the more he does, the less and less time she spends at home, and ultimately, the less time she finds for her husband.

So we in this society are developing a breed of very frustrated husbands, who no longer can have sex with their wives when they want to. In addition, when they are both at home, she often claims to be too tired to make love, and is often more grumpy than being loving and lovely.

So the man, who only wants a simple life of going out to work, then coming home to his family, a meal on the table, his clothes cleaned, and to make love to his wife, now finds that his world has been forcibly complicated by the government and the feminist movement.

He no longer sees his family as often as he used to. In addition, he now has to cook his own food and wash his own clothes. Added to that, his wife is often not available to make love when he wants to. As a result, life for many husbands and male partners has become very sour indeed.

Recent surveys show that fewer men than in the 1990's think that it is best for women to go out to work. The figure then was close to 50 per cent. Now that figure is closer to 40 per cent.

Many men, especially those with wealth, now think twice before taking on a female partner as the wife. The man now prefers to keep her as a partner and not get married—having a woman for sexual gratification when he wants it or not having one at all.

In the past, when marriage was the norm after getting involved with each other, today, living in sin has become more acceptable for both parties. One of the results of this kind of a loose lifestyle is that sexually transmitted diseases are inexorably on the rise with no end or turn for the better in sight.

Also on the rise are incidences of teenage pregnancies and single parenthood. As long as we are set on the course we have, a course that we as a society have chosen, there will be no turning back the trend, despite the best efforts from the government's end. The government will always be playing catch-up as it chases its tail because their policies on the family are all wrong and misguided. Then the book that many of us despise, the Bible, will be proved right time and time again.

Well, the changes fostered on society, whereby the husband is no longer the sole breadwinner, but both husband and wife now earn a wage, has not worked successfully in most cases.

Despite trying to make ends meet, families now find that they have to make a choice between paying the bills and feeding the mouths in need. So instead of having a surplus from two wages, they find themselves in more financial debt, which is now the biggest crisis in ages.

One of the results of this is that couples have become unhappier than ever before. So as they become unhappy, they pull further apart as bickering, discontentment, and divisions set in. The fact that they both work keeps them apart more often than they wish anyhow. And unhappiness brought on by our long-hours work culture, while still not getting enough to make ends meet, pulls them even further apart indeed. So money does not necessarily bring happiness. In most cases, it brings with it unhappiness.

Happiness and a strong family life are more important than any amount of money that you might acquire. So before you rush headlong to make what is often only a few more pennies, think about your family and where it might lead you all to. *Don't let money take away what it cannot buy.*

If you have a lot of time to spend with your family, or even a small amount of time, treasure it with all your life, because throwing it away to keep up with the Joneses could cost you your life or at least the good life you once had. It is nearly always better for one of you to work and the other to stay home to look after the children.

Putting yourself last for the sake of your family will ultimately make you into a well-rounded and happier person.

If you think that you have gone too far down the road of trying to keep up with the Joneses, and there is no way out other than work, work, and work till you drop, think again. The last thing that you want to do is drop, so there must be a way out, and there is a way out of the quagmire of debt and family disintegration. Because when you drop, your wife's next husband will be congratulating you on being such a successful executive for him now to benefit.

Children

The mad rush to get women doing what men traditionally did and men doing what women traditionally did, thus trying to make everyone the same, which is not possible, has got children squeezed in the middle by parents who no longer have the time and space for them. More and more, children now find that they are fending for themselves, as there is no one around to guide them. To make matters worse, the government makes it near impossible to discipline children properly when they go astray.

Some children of a young age now spend more time in school and with childminders than they spend with their parents or with at least one of their parents. So as parents pull apart from each other due to work pressures and the resulting unhappy relationships, they inevitably pull away from their children too. Sometimes during a whole year, the only quality time that children and parents get with each other is a couple of weeks in the summer and at Christmas.

As a result, children also become disoriented, discontented, and unhappy. The onset of trouble in children's lives as well as for parents and society at large begins to take shape. Children are very impressionable creatures, and too often, they are left to deal with society's deep-seated troubles and confusing influences on their own.

One area in which these confusing influences and society's deep-seated troubles come to the fore is the arena of television and computers. As children are allowed to remain more and more unoccupied, they are dragged in more and more by what they see on the box. And what is shown on the box is more and more unsuited for some adults, let alone children. They are allowed to watch violence, swearing, sex, and anything that keeps people hooked. Children can also talk to anyone they wish to on the Internet.

They are kept away from talking to strangers or being on their own with strangers in the streets, mainly by keeping them locked indoors. However, indoors, on the Internet they are allowed to talk to strangers, be on their own with whomever they want to, and do whatever they want to. How ironical? Yet which practice is much more dangerous? That is the level of stupidity we, as a society, have sunk to.

Even more ironical and downright stupid is the fact that many children are allowed to talk to anyone on the Internet, even pedophiles, with or without their mothers' knowledge, but they are not allowed to talk to their fathers, as some mothers use their children as pawns in their game of hurting their other half.

The programmers of television have long worked out that what keeps children and adults hooked, are not things which are wholesome and good, but all that's bad, evil and vile dressed up in style in our society and world today. So they look, listen and learn from the wrong sources and earn for themselves and society at some later stage what we have sown in their lives this day and age; as parents tend to other things deemed more important at the time than the family thing.

Other parents, still, sit with their kids as they watch these programmes, while feeding them with the most damaging food possible. Not only do they sit for hours in front of the box to create an obese culture, but the fast food on top also ensures that whatever weight is put on as result of prolonged sitting is added to by what is eaten.

As parents become too busy for their children, they have no time to cook for them either. So today there are many children who do not know what it is to eat good food and have proper meals. Many of them are so used to eating junk, that when presented with something good and wholesome, they refuse it. It then becomes a battle to change their eating habits, by which time it may be too late anyway.

Not only do they not know what it is to eat good food, but many don't know how to cook good food either, as they are not trained at home to cook. Once again parents are often too busy for that. It is often left to schools to pick up where the parents have failed.

It follows that if they do not know how to cook, they don't do much around the house either, apart from making a mess. This is how many of our youngsters are brought up today.

They make a mess, and when you ask them to clean up after themselves, they pay you little or no mind at all or a lot of lip service instead. This is because they know that they cannot be forced to do anything, as there is no stick to follow. So they do what they like. They can choose to do what their parents ask, or they can refuse. And more and more they are choosing to refuse. They know that the balance of power has shifted from the parents to the children, so they choose to push parents as far as they can—often threatening to call the police if the parents lay on them, a hand.

These are some of the changes that the left has fostered on families and the country as a whole to herald in a new age of 'progress' and better times for society's soul. Under Thatcherism there was, 'no such thing as society'. Under New Labour the soul of the country has grown so cold, that stability has been replaced by ASBOS, benefits or aborted babies, bankers, bankruptcies and broken families.

Children and young people now take their lawlessness to the streets, so anyone who speaks to them like a parent can expect to face the consequences, as was the case in Croydon recently.

A young girl who dropped paper on the street after eating her meal was asked by a police officer to pick it up. Result: she and her colleagues set up on the police officer and gave her a 'good going-over'.

In another instance, youths smoking on a train were spoken to by a female passenger, who asked them to put the cigarettes out. Result: she was pushed on to the line below and sustained injuries as a result. But more significantly, she could have lost her life, if there had been an oncoming train. So could the police constable mentioned earlier have lost her life, too.

But even worse than this, youths are killing each other, using knives in cities all around the United Kingdom today, and in a desperate attempt to close the gate once the horses have started bolting, the government is resorting to knee-jerk measures to halt the rise in knife crime. The government puts the onus on children for the results of their actions while taking no account of its policies toward families.

As a result, it is sad to say, there is a lot more of this type of behaviour to come, resulting from blinkered policies towards families. Parents no longer have the time and/or the will to bring their children up properly under current circumstances. So we have the influences of television, Internet, video games, peer pressure, alcohol, sex and drugs taking over.

And it so happens, whether by coincidence or design, that just as the government has made it more difficult for parents to bring up children, it has become a lot easier over the past ten years or so to access loose, violent, and immoral material on the Internet, television, and on video games. Next to this, alcohol and drugs have become cheaper. The government's downgrading of certain drugs to class C seems to be a package of measures aimed at the vulnerable, which the children are. It's as if they are saying, 'Take your pick or the lot, if you like'.

In addition, we have the tax, housing, and benefit policies aimed at promoting single parenthood and destroying marriage and co-habitation. I can assure you that there is now a crisis, as children do like these newly found circumstances. They see them as a license to run riot with immorality, not caring a penny for anyone in authority.

In such circumstances, how does one expect parents to cope? Likewise, how does anybody expect children to cope, let alone know better, when adults who are responsible for policy-making seem to know not what they are really doing to families in this country? The terrible result of their reckless experiments and their knee-jerk reaction once things go wrong is clear evidence that they don't.

What policy-makers have done to our children with their decade-long policy changes in liberalising most things and destroying traditional values, is like placing a very young child in the kitchen, often on his own with the fire on, and saying, 'You are on your own. Your mother is busy trying to earn a penny and your father is dizzy from drink and drug at the local pub.'

You would not put a young child in the kitchen on his own, let alone a baby. But that is exactly what our government, which claims to know what's good for us, has done.

Children learn what they live and live what they learn. They do not know right from wrong. We have to teach them that. So if you leave a young child in the kitchen on his own, with the cooker on, sooner or later his eagerness to learn more will draw him to touch the hotpot or the fire, and we all know the consequences of that. With things as they are now, I am almost certain that hospitals are dealing with increasing problems of burns to children today.

The child will open the drawer to inquire about what is in there, and he will take out one or more implements to experiment with and draw his own conclusions about what they do. He might have been taught by his parents not to go in the kitchen. So he may well be hiding and peeping while quietly experimenting with items he should not yet be experimenting with.

If there is more than one child in the kitchen on their own, the problems of likely injury increases as children become more mischievous when they are together in groups. So we don't leave our children alone in the kitchen.

If the child or children are in the kitchen with one parent, then the job of that parent becomes more difficult than if she had the other parent to help out. So although the child is less likely to harm himself, he is still more likely to do so than if there were two parents around to help.

So when the government puts the pressure on both parents to go out to work coupled with promoting single parenthood over two parents and marriage, they effectively tell the children to learn about life on their own, at school or with a childminder. Never mind the parents—they don't matter as much as they used to and the father certainly doesn't count anymore.

When children are left on their own or with one parent, coupled with the pressures of life today, they are being forced to grow up quicker and earlier than they should. And the pressures of life today can be likened to leaving children in the kitchen on their own or with one parent. And children are getting burnt in increasing numbers from what they have learnt while being left to their own devices.

Credit Crunch

*T*he credit crunch has served to hand more severe blows to families and men alike.

Now when poor families lose their homes, they are often not able to get housing in the private sector because of the children factor and the damage they might cause to the landlord's property.

So they have to rely on the council or the housing associations. In the past, your needs were considered urgent if you were a family, so you would go to the top of the housing waiting list, but now if you are a family, this is no longer the case. The family component is now a hindrance to you getting housing, because of the husband. Take the husband out of the equation, and then you go straight to the top of the housing waiting list.

How irrelevant husbands and men have become in our society today! With examples like this, what incentive is there for a man to get involved with a woman, let alone get married?

Now if a man wants to see his wife and his children he has to play hide and seek when approaching the home in the hope that no one in authority spots him, or she and the children could lose their precious possession—the home, possibly a one-bedroom house from the council.

This is another example of how difficult life for men have become in this country under socialist rule.

Though these changes work against us men, don't resist them. Grow stronger through change and, 'We get up and keep going.' 146.

Max Gunther quipped, 'When you are in a tug-of-war with a tiger, give him the rope before he gets to your arm. You can always buy a new rope!' Resistance to change just creates ulcers, sleeplessness and stress. So here are some attitudes you may need to adjust. Stop thinking like a victim, expecting others to rescue you, feel sorry for you or reduce your stress levels.

Get behind the wheel of your own life! You're not helpless, and the situation is not hopeless. God's word promises you 'can do everything ... with the help of Christ'. 147. Then stop deciding not to change. Instead of banging your head against the wall of reality, invest your efforts into changing what you can—such as your attitude and your approach!

It takes more energy to hang on to old habits and beliefs than to embrace new ones. Stop playing the new game by the old rules. When a car that's stuck in second gear keeps trying to do 100mph, guess what happens—meltdown! If you don't want to burn out, learn to change gears. When your life's seasons, assignments or relationships change, begin to adjust.

Learn to play by the new rules, otherwise you'll keep losing. Stop trying to control the uncontrollable. When the music changes, it's time to learn some new dance steps, otherwise you will finish up sitting on the sidelines. You may not like the change, but you can learn to flow with them. 'We are perplexed ... but we don't give up and quit ... We get knocked down, but we get up again and keep going.' 148. (**Source: UCB's The Word for Today**).

The Weakest Link

The problems caused by a decade of broken homes will be long and lasting. For one, a child growing up in a dysfunctional home where there is only one parent loses the love and care of the other parent. So they will not know what it is like to have, what is in most cases, a loving and caring father. Their views of life will be slanted towards mum's view of the way things should be. They may develop a hostile attitude towards men as a result, and this is not confined to girls.

Because one link in the chain is missing, namely the father and in a few cases the mother, their upbringing may be quite unstable leading to an unstable lifestyle and unbalanced thinking. The absence of one parent can and has in many cases been very damaging to many children, leaving them very angry and frustrated. Another by-product of single parenthood is sometimes short-term, as well as long-term damage to children's mental and or physical health due to smoke, sex, drink, or drugs, or the lot.

So these children, when they become adults, are more likely to be single parents themselves because they will inevitably have difficulty forming and sustaining a long-term relationship. Their view of life as a child will be reflected in how they relate to their partner.

They did not have love from one parent, so they often have difficulty showing love to their partner, if that partner is of the same sex as the absent parent. They will relate to their partner in the same way they related to the absent parent, which is often with anger and derision. They will expect to be treated in the same way as their single parent who brought them up did, and this is reflected, among other ways, by constantly referring favourably back to the parent who brought them up.

So without realising it, they expect that partner in their life to fill the role of the parent they did not have by constantly putting their partner down and expecting and demanding more from him or her. It is usually the man who is on the receiving end of such verbal assaults.

This does not bode well either for the children they may be bringing up and for the public purse. Because single parenthood breeds more and more dysfunctional families, they will cost the taxpayer more and more in benefits, hospital admissions for abortions etc, treatment centres for drugs and alcohol, prison places, and so on.

As a result, we will end up with more and more communities where the financial cost to the taxpayer outweighs the financial contribution these families and these communities make to society. It may not be intended that way by the government, but that is the net result of liberal family policies. This is the result of the blind leading the blind, as neither knows what he or she is truly doing. The government and other policymakers are confident and elated when putting these policies in peoples faces but become sarcastic and unrealistic when these very policies go ballistic.

The idea at the outset that single-parent families are just as effective as two-parent families has been proven, over the past decade or so, to be a big lie and nothing more than dogma and a foolish and reckless experiment that has inevitably gone wrong before long. A chain is only as strong as its weakest link, and that applies to families also if you only stop to think. These families are now weeping and reaping the full wrath of Labour's malign thinking. Many no longer eat proper meals like their grandparents once did, but instead suck on sour grapes—the fruit and full force of Labour's dreadful mistakes.

Be Smart, Act Smart, and Not Like a Go-kart

*R*adical change is nearly always never good, unless you are guided by the word and Spirit of God. Ask anyone who has gone through a divorce, if they are happier when the dust has settled, or did it ever settle, as a result of their decisions? Look at countries that have started wars and gone through revolutions. Are they any better off as a result? In cases like these, people usually jump from the frying pan straight into the fire and it takes years, sometimes decades, for that fire to quench and for things to start settling down.

And when they settle down, they usually start from a position well below the position they were in when the conflict started in the first place. Not only are they poorer for their experience, they also carry extended years, decades, and centuries of hate, resentment and bitterness.

So if you are thinking of divorce, you might well be thinking of the horrors you want to leave behind and hopes of joy and fulfillment that a new relationship might bring. But look a little deeper.

The financial commitment would be divided among your previous partner, your children, and your new partner, and possibly her children too. Can you afford that? Your new partner might want greater financial commitment and security from you. Your previous partner might be 'taking you to the cleaners.'

You could become frustrated in your job because you cannot meet your financial commitments. Your partner could become frustrated with you because you cannot meet her financial needs. You may also find that the financial climate at the time is affecting your job or your business. You may even be made redundant or sacked for not taking due care and attention in your job because of all the worries on you mind.

One partner has given you the boot and the other one could be talking about doing the same too. History has a way of repeating itself. Humans are very good at that and far less good at not making the same mistakes twice. Though you grind a fool in a motor with a pestle along with crushed grain, Yet his foolishness will not depart from him. 127.

Your new partner may be carrying a lot of baggage from a previous relationship, and so will you from your previous relationship.

Your children will miss you terribly and you will miss them too. How are you going to cope with so many different scenarios? When there is chaos, which is what often happens at the end of one relationship and the beginning of another, there seems to be one trap after another for you, and one hole after another to fall into. And when emotions are high, you do fall from one hole into another. As soon as you find your footing again, the rug is being pulled from under feet once more. And the downward spiral never seems to come to an end.

What seemed sweet to you in the beginning may ends up souring you.

If your relationship is not working, no matter what you try, jumping straight into another one is often not the solution. For one, you don't know what you are jumping into. All that glitters is not gold.

Why not take time out, reflect, and take things slowly before making decisions you might regret. In the time you take to reflect, you will be building back your financial resources instead of splitting them into several different directions. This is what will happen if you take on another partner, or even worse still, another family.

With more time to yourself, God will reveal a lot of things to you, which would not be the case if your energy were all over the place. You will learn more about your previous partner and the opposite sex in general and this will put you in good stead for any future relationship.

The heart of the prudent **acquires** knowledge, And the ear of the wise **seek** knowledge. 128. When it comes to staying teachable understand two things:

1) *Nothing is interesting until you are interested.* Philip B. Crosby writes: 'There is a theory of human that says **people subconsciously retard their own growth.** They come to rely on clichés and habits. Once they reach the age of their own personal comfort with the world, they stop learning and their minds run on idle for the rest of their days. They may progress organizationally, they may be ambitious and eager, and they may even work night and day, but they learn no more.'

   It's a tragedy when we allow ourselves to get in a rut and never climb out. We miss the best God has to offer. In contrast, teachable people are fully engaged in life. They get excited about things. They are interested in discovery, discussion, application and growth.

2) *Successful people view learning differently than those who are unsuccessful.* That doesn't mean that unsuccessful people are unable to think the way successful people do. If you have the desire and the discipline, you can retrain yourself to think differently. Teachable people are always open to new ideas. And are willing to learn from anyone who has something to offer.

Sydney J. Harris wrote: '**A winner knows how much he still has to learn,** even when he is considered an expert by others. A loser wants to be considered an expert by others, before he has learned enough to know how little he knows.' It's all a matter of attitude. Bottom line—it's truly remarkable how much a person has to learn, before he realises how little he knows. So, stay teachable. (**Source: UCB's The Word for Today**).

You will also learn things about yourself that you did not know before. All this will help you in the future and help you prevent the same mistakes you made in the past. Ideas and opportunities will open themselves up to you when you have time to reflect, thus helping you to make better choices in the future. Also, write down the things that make sense. You might even be able to write a book. Sort out things such as your finances, your paperwork, your laundry, and anything else that was left to fester while your life was being slowly destroyed.

In this way your life will be rebuilt slowly, sometimes rapidly, which will not be the case if you take on more burdens, responsibilities and frustrations with your newly found situation. One scenario will show that you are learning, hence you will start growing. The other will show that you have not learnt anything and you will continue descending to an awful ending.

If you do not leave the family home, but decide instead to tough it out, there is no point in withdrawing your services completely or carrying on as if things have not changed. That would be counterproductive, and it would give your partner more ammunition to get even worse or use your complete withdrawal against you in more ways than one. He or she has changed for the worse. That is what you have to face up to.

There is no point trying to do better to placate him or her when you can clearly see that they are getting worse. That will eventually sap your morale, making you even more frustrated in the end. This could also cause serious physical and/or mental health problems for you when that person has driven you into the ground or, even worse, into a pit. It could even lead to your committing suicide or harming your partner.

A far smarter way to approach a worsening situation is to withdraw some of your services, so you alter your approach, as he or she alters theirs. The worse they get, the more you withdraw. The divergence will become greater and greater till eventually, they will feel the pinch and realise that what they are doing to you is, in fact, harming themselves too.

When they see that their workload has increased or that the money they have at their disposal is gradually drying up, they will soon think twice about their approach to you. For instance, they will start to bite their lips before they allow something nasty to fly out at you.

As soon as improvement begins, convergence can resume; so once they calm down, you can restart normal services gradually. Or once you stop doing the work you used to do for them, they will realise that they are losing out and start pulling their weight. You do not have to say a word because actions speak louder than words. The change in you is what will motivate them to change too.

This is far better than arguing and engaging in a bitter feud, which harms everyone, or trying to do your best in an impossible mess. You have been given one mouth, two eyes, two ears, two hands and two feet. Speak less, look and listen more, and do more to heal the sore.

Who has ever been motivated to do better by someone who keeps putting them down and telling them how 'bad' and 'useless' they are? The answer is no one. You are more likely to be motivated to do something bad through anger that develops as a result of what is being said to you or about you. Instead of doing something that you might regret, walk away from the fire and retire to your room. Do not allow yourself to be burnt.

Go away, think smart, and act smart. Advocate altering your approach and see the results and benefits, instead of reaping the wreckage of reckless discourse and decisions.

Counselling

I don't advocate counselling in most cases because such situations are often an opportunity for one party to let rip and the other party getting hung out to dry. Also, quite often in the heat of the moment, the counsellor takes sides when at the outset he or she says that they would not take sides and are only there to mediate.

This can cause one party to feel really bruised and think that he or she has been unjustly treated. This creates more resentment and more problems than it solves. Some people go into counselling with ulterior motives. Instead of going in with an open mind to receive help, they enter this scenario to get their own way at all costs, expecting the other party to capitulate as they humiliate.

There are many fault-finders in our world. The worse they are, the least they can find it in themselves to say sorry when they are at fault. They are usually always at it, and the more you hang around with them, the worse they get, and the worse you get too. A righteous man who falters before the wicked is like a murky spring and a polluted well. 81. A prudent man foresees evil and hides himself; The simple pass on and are punished. 82.

You are like a football that gets kicked to a pulp. And ask them to say sorry at any point—no chance. They are also usually puffed up, full of pride, and rarely happy.

This is very common in relationships that have grown stale, so familiarity sets in, and familiarity breeds contempt. In these types of relationships, situations usually get from bad to worse, and if not arrested, one party will snap—with sometimes catastrophic results. So alter your course before your partner alters you.

In altering your approach, remember to stay on the high road. Don't withdraw your services entirely; don't try to get even, such as complaining to others about your partner (unless you are confiding in a friend and counsellor), or hitting him or her physically. Don't rub your partner up the wrong way. Keep your approach measured to achieve specific aims. If you pull too much in one direction, you may reach the bursting point and it would be difficult to repair the relationship. So don't be quick-tempered. A quick-tempered man acts foolishly. 83 . . . the prudent considers well his steps. 84. He who is slow to wrath has great understanding, but he who is impulsive exalts folly. 85.

Be like an elastic band; be flexible, pull a bit in the right direction so as not to cause damage, but enough to induce pain. There is no gain without pain. And when you stop pulling, watch your relationship heal and things repair themselves as the elastic band springs back into place having served its purpose.

So whatever you do, your aim should be to heal your marriage, not to break it. So many people who have divorced wished they never went down that route, because the damage to them and their family is far worse than they ever anticipated. That is like the elastic band that snaps, as pride goes before the fall, thus exalting folly.

On the other hand, if you allow your marriage to heal, the renewal is often so uplifting that you can scarcely believe you were recently at loggerheads, and all your efforts to renew your relationship will be worth it. Pride goes before destruction, and a haughty spirit before a fall. 86. How much better to get wisdom than gold . . . 87. When a man's ways please the Lord, He makes even his enemies to be at peace with him. 88.

But for all this to work, you need to have patience. Rome was not built in a day. If you keep to the high ground, one day your enemies will see the

Lord reward your efforts with an increase in prosperity and happiness. You will reap the rewards of your labour, if you don't give up through impulsive behaviour, which you will regret to your death.

How much better it is to reap the sweet smell of success, through staying the course of a long, hard slog, than harvest a life of all kinds of thorns, through short-sightedness, hastiness and strife. Shortsightedness leads to long-term damage, destruction, disease, and even death as some would attest, had they been here to talk of the mess that they would not or could not redress.

Stay the course of time, and time will stay with you. Move away from time, and time will run out for you, leaving you and yours in a senseless mess. Then allow God to be the great healer that He is. This is better than any course of counselling. Put God first and everything else will follow. You are far more likely to live happier and longer lives then. In addition, men in marriage live longer than single men or those cohabiting.

Marriages That Work and Lifestyles That Don't

*M*arriages that work are those that stand the test of time no matter what the temptation, the provocation, or complication. Marriages that work are also usually those that stem from middle-class and upper class backgrounds, and often those in suburban and rural communities. And marriages that work best are those from Christian backgrounds.

So needless to say, if you want to have a successful marriage, aspire to be in these categories if you are not, and do the things that these people do. Anything else is likely to end in failure and a poverty-stricken existence, as the many statistics in this area will show you.

Some of things that middle-class people do, which are going out of fashion elsewhere in society, is having a faith and going to church. Some may say, 'What has that got to do with having a successful relationship?' Well, the fact is that having a strong faith in God helps enormously in preserving one's marriage and leading a happier and more satisfied existence, whether you like to hear that or not. The fear of God is the beginning of wisdom . . . 89, and people in successful marriages are usually God-fearing people.

But don't take my word for it. Go back to the many statistics over the years that bear this fact out. Knowing this fact, why then would anyone want to live any other form of existence, which has proven to bring only misery in the end?

But humans are strange creatures that are capable of amazing levels of madness, stupidity, and immaturity in forming what to them are sane beliefs. Let no one deceive himself. If anyone among you seems to be wise in this age, let him become a fool that he may become wise. 90.

Some such beliefs are, 'if I sleep around I won't get hurt, and I won't hurt anyone else. I won't have a baby. I am likely to be happier. I will be fulfilling my needs.'

'If I don't get married, I will live a safer, more secure, and more satisfied existence, no strings attached, and my man will stick around anyhow.' But when this does not work, which in most cases it does not, people think, 'I can have multiple baby fathers.' When people cohabit-ate, one party usually has no wish to spend the rest of his life with the other partner, so he or she has no desire to marry. The ties are more easily broken then and they often do.

Then some say, 'if I have different baby fathers, I will get looked after and things will be better for the children and me.' 'The government will step in to help me', which, sad to say, is true. The government supports this type of behaviour by pumping more and more money into single parenthood, while marriage gets little or no support. In fact, marriage gets torn down wherever and whenever left wing forces can.

Knowing this fact, some say, 'I don't need a man anyhow. The government will look after my kids and me.' So they show their man the door. What kind of society is this that promotes these types of values?

Another thing that happens less in middle-class homes than in working-class homes is domestic violence. This behaviour happens more also in homes where the couples are not married. So why would anyone opt for a lifestyle where this is more likely?

Also more likely in working-class homes are scenarios where the children turn around and abuse their parents verbally and physically, showing less respect all round. This happens more often also in cohabiting households and single-parent households than in marriage households.

Income levels in marriages and in middle-class homes are more stable and tend to increase more over time than in cohabiting or single-parent households, where income levels tend to be erratic and even fall over time. This is partly caused by too many mouths to feed and too many problems to face up to financially, physically, mentally and spiritually.

More time is spent in trying to sort out your many problems and finding that you are actually going backwards, instead of focusing on and building on your achievements, had you been married and in a stable relationship in the first place. So if you behave as though you know it all, you will fall.

Stay teachable. One of the paradoxes of life is that the things which initially make you successful, are not necessarily the things that keep you successful. You have to remain open to new ideas and be willing to learn new skills. Dr J Konrad Hole says: 'If you cannot be teachable, having talent wont help you. If you cannot be flexible, having a goal won't help you. If you cannot be grateful, having abundance won't help you. If you cannot be mentor-able, having a future won't help you. If you cannot be durable, having a plan won't help you.'

Confined to a dungeon and facing the certainty of an executioner's chopping block, Paul writes to Timothy and asks him to bring: a) writing paper. 'I still have something to say' b) books. 'I still have more to learn' 129. Learning should be your lifelong pursuit.

The Roman scholar Cato started to study Greek when he was 80. When asked why he was tackling such a difficult task at his age he replied, 'It's the earliest age I have left.' Unlike Cato, too many of us regard learning as an event instead of a process. It's estimated that only one third of all adults read an entire book after their graduation. Why? Because they view education as a *period of life*, not a way of life.

Learning is an activity that is not restricted by age. Every stage of life presents lessons to be learned. We can choose to be teachable and continue to learn them, or we can be closed-minded and stop growing. The decision is ours. (Source: UCB's The Word for Today).

Think about it. If you think that marriage needs too much work and creates too many problems that you might not be able to get out of, the problems you find if you were to divorce or live in a cohabiting relationship are far greater in comparison. I am yet to meet a happily divorced couple. Maybe there are some, but I have not met any. Compare that to the many happily married couples around.

The fact that marriages last much longer than cohabiting relationships is a story in itself. Marriages have stood the test of time and should be cherished and promoted as the basis of a stable and successful society.

It is ludicrous to promote anything else, and the statistics over the past decade have proven that. Promoting other forms of lifestyles has opened a Pandora's box of problems that the government spends all its time in trying to tackle and fix but ends up going backwards with a litany of failures, instead.

There can be no other outcome if what you sow has never proven successful in the first place. But instead, they sow in hope rather than sow in what has stood the test of time and proven very successful, though unpopular, and which is the only viable way forward. So from being hopeful for the success of their policies, they in fact become hope-fools experimenting with fire and what could be called explosives, as it has backfired in no uncertain terms. And society is left to pick up the pieces. The recent street riots are the latest examples of this colossal failure in policy.

Because some people want to go down that road, the authorities are following fashion with what has proven to be a failure rather than following something that is solid, strengthening, sound, of substance, and beneficial for all concerned, including the wider community.

The other ways being promoted rely heavily on one's selfish motives, or self-preservation, but often end up destroying all concerned. If you are not married, you are more likely to go for the 'easy' options in the relationship such as walking away, abusing your partner, and/or your children. You are also less likely to want to make things work for you both.

While if you are married, you are more likely to be more measured in your approach, should a crisis arise. And if you survive it, your relationship will, in most cases, be stronger and better for the experience. Your experience will enable you to learn from your mistakes and be a better husband or wife.

But if you keep walking away from relationship to relationship, no learning is taking place and you are actually getting from bad to worse without realising it. You will, in all probability, be justifying yourself in all your behaviour. And the worse you get, the more self-justification and excuses you find for you actions.

If you stay put in your relationship, what you are doing may not seem to be the right thing, as your character is tested sometimes to the limit, but I promise you, you will be doing the right thing, not just for yourself, but for your family and society as a whole.

And you in turn will benefit from seeing your children being stable, well rounded citizens and not becoming a part of the criminal justice system or seeing them become a part of the high youth unemployment rate, or seeing them spreading their seed and having children while being children themselves.

In addition you will be playing your part in not becoming a victim of mugging and violence from a wayward teenager somewhere along life's paths.

When the dust is settled, you will be glad you did the right thing. You will be able to see your children at Christmas, birthdays, and times that matter, if not all the time. They will come to see you and look after you when you have grown old. So instead of leading a lonely, miserable existence, you will lead a happy and fulfilled life.

Your life will feel a lot more fulfilled when you think that you have done all you could to keep the marriage and keep the family together, rather than jumping ship at the first sign that things have slipped.

'...whatever things are true, whatever things are noble, whatever things are just, whatever things are pure, whatever things are lovely, whatever things are of good report. If there is any virtue and if there is anything praiseworthy—meditate on these things.' (Philippians 4:8).

If in doubt about your relationship, think about the things that your partner has done for you in the past and the things he or she has done for the children. Think of the things that he or she has not done in the interest of the marriage, such as not being unfaithful. Saying you love someone and doing things that show you love someone are two different things. So think about the good things instead of what you perceive to be things wrong with your marriage, and the light will begin to shine in your thoughts, thus taking away the darkness, which often does not matter as much as the accent you place on it.

In most cases, single parenthood is, as we all know from a decade and more of left-wing rule, a disaster and an exercise in mediocrity, causing people with more well-ordered lives having to pick up the pieces to prevent a complete collapse of society. And they do this primarily through the taxes they pay, which go into benefits or, as is often the case, soaking up the effects of crime and antisocial behaviour. We all know which group in society are the main perpetrators of crime and antisocial behaviour, unless you are in denial.

So are you too B-U-S-Y for your FAMILY?
....THAT SATAN MIGHT NOT OUTWIT US...91.

Addressing a worldwide convention of demons, Satan told them:'As long as Christians stay close to God we've no power over them, so:

1) Keep them busy with non-essentials.
2) Tempt them to overspend and go into debt.
3) Make them work long hours to maintain empty lifestyles.
4) Discourage them from spending family time, for when homes disintegrate there is no refuge from work.
5) Over stimulate their minds with television and computers so that they can't hear God speaking to them.
6) Fill their coffee tables and nightstands with newspapers and magazines so they have no time for bible reading.
7) Flood their letter boxes with sweepstakes, promotions and get-rich-quick schemes; keep them chasing material things.
8) Put glamorous models on television and on magazine covers to keep them focused on outward appearances; that way they will be dissatisfied with themselves and their mates.
9) Make sure couples are too exhausted for physical intimacy; that way they will be tempted to look elsewhere.
10) Emphasise Santa and the Easter Bunny; that way you'll divert them from the real meaning of the holidays.
11) Involve them in 'good' causes so they wont have time for 'eternal' ones.
12) Make them self-sufficient. Keep them so busy working in their own strength that they will never know the joy of God's power working through them.
13) Keep them in the pleasures of this world such as smoking, drinking, and sexual immorality, leading to cancer, cirrhosis, and sexual explosives.

Do these thirteen things faithfully, I promise—it'll work!'

Have you figured out the difference between being busy and being successful in what God's called you to do?

Sometimes being B-U-S-Y just means *Being Under Satan's Yoke!* (**Source: UCB's The Word for Today**).

Doing these thirteen things faithfully also means <u>B</u>eing <u>U</u>nder <u>S</u>wamp <u>Y</u>early, sinking deeper and deeper, surely. What a waste of large sections of the human race, who make themselves a certainty of sinking into eternity, where there is even more mess to digest, certainly. Why not get out of that mess you are in by finding the steps out of that swampy bin. It is a difficult climb to begin, when the weight and mess you are carrying from that swamp is sin. But if you begin you are guaranteed to win if the steps you use are the bible's route out of sin and suttee, and that swampy waste bin.

Falling into the swamp that made your life this sordid mess does not make you the failure that some detest, but quitting in the swamp thing thus failing to find the steps upwards and outwards is the killer that and slayer that keeps you away from your eternal maker.

A week without God makes one weak, as one is trapped in the swamp and sleaze indeed. So on Christ, the solid rock, I stand, because all other ground is sinking sand.

Statistics from the World Health Organisation show that:

* In any given year, about 20% of adolescents will experience a mental health problem, most commonly depression or anxiety.
* About 16 million girls aged 15 to 19 years give birth every year—roughly 11% of all births worldwide.
* Nearly two-thirds of premature deaths . . . are associated with conditions or behaviours that begin in their youth, including: tobacco use, lack of physical activity, unprotected sex or exposure to violence.

Statistics from a Unicef report, in 2007, ranked Britain:

- *bottom* out of 21 developed countries for child welfare.
- *3rd from bottom* for educational standards.
- *Bottom* for self-esteem.
- *2nd from bottom* for teenage pregnancies.
- Children *significantly less likely to be in two-parent families* than in other developed countries.

These are dreadful facts of life in our world, as well as in Britain today, where suicides and teenage violence have also been on the up. That is what thirteen years of socialism and feminism has brought us to, while at the same time people have been putting the bible in the bin.

While you choose to abandon Him for the pleasures of sin, remember: **sin's pleasures are always shared, but their dreadful consequences are so dear, they must be suffered alone.** You lose your short-lived sinful glory, and what is left are life-long Shame, Losses, Aches and Pains. That is the SLAP that Satan serves for serving him, instead of resisting and cursing his sinful waste bin.

When wealth is gone, little is lost; when health is gone something is lost; but when character is gone, all is lost. What about when all three are gone?!! Then Christ is a must.

They say, Lord, you do not exist. Somehow I believed all this. Then I had to come to this hellish place, before I could see your saving face.

God is not to be mocked: what we sow, we are certain to reap.

Eternity is a certainty; make your choice, therefore, the side of Happiness, Eternal Life and resulting Peace. So why not seek God's HELP, instead of a sleepy and comfortable acceptance of the Horrors of Excesses and Loose Living, where many have been sold into the enemy's fold?

The inspiration I get to write so prophetically is not of my own. I operate on God's higher plane and not in man's domain.

Looking Back at Lessons Learnt

When a problem arises, deal with it there and then and do not allow it to fester. Festering means other things will come along and crowd it out. Then the danger is that the problem will rear its ugly head again, the sore will burst, or it will almost be too late to deal effectively with it.

This could be an unpaid bill that the bank slaps charges on you for, or an unpaid utility bill, which the utility company cut its service to you for, or something worse, such as a health problem that you have been too busy to deal with. Think about it.

One of main reasons problems develop is that one is too busy to look after oneself, one's affairs, and one's family properly. Take regular time out of your busy schedule to look after things that don't seem to matter that much, but if left unattended, could lead to disaster, putting it mildly.

Now think again. 'What if I tended to my affairs properly and in good time?' At the end of it, you would feel a lot more at ease and there would be less pressure felt, including blood pressure. This would be better than running around most times like a headless chicken, often achieving very little but increasing your stress levels instead, and resulting in slow but sure damage being done to your life in more areas than you may be aware of.

You would start to enjoy life more because you will be more relaxed and contended, knowing that everything is in place and in the way they should be. Also, as time moves on, you will start making it a habit of looking after things in good time because you found the last experience so fulfilling and rewarding. Not only that, you will also start to do things properly, if you hardly ever did things this way in the past. You will have the time to spare to do things well.

It is so nice sitting back and listening to some classical music, for example, knowing that everything in life is sorted out. And if everything is not sorted, you can seek the advice of an older and often wiser head.

If you have little experience of life, it is not wise to ignore the advice of an older and often wiser head. Before throwing their advice down the drain, at least go away and think about it in a calmer state of mind. You will be pleasantly surprised at what their advice will reveal to you, after what initially looked like interference or rubbish. Allow the advice to run its course in time, then it will be clearer that what was said was fed to bring you fresh and sweet smelling bread. If in doubt seek the advice of other friends before making your mind up. Without counsel, plans go awry, but in a multitude of counsellors they are established. 92. By wise counsel you will wage your own war, and in a multitude of counsellors there is safety. 93.

If many young people had listened to their parents' advice, they would be in a much better position today, and many of them will confess this to you. Also, the world would be a better place too. One has got to remember that parents talk from experience that younger folks won't necessarily have.

Another benefit of taking time out to sort things out in your life is that when you do so, your eyes will be opened up to things you never thought were there, as well as to possibilities you never thought of or thought were improbable. A whole new world could be opened up to you, possibly getting you away from a cluttered and depressed lifestyle.

He who covers his sins do it out of fear, and therefore will live with fear and live in fear and torment—oh dear, oh dear!

The price he pays is and will continue to be dear. And the more he sins, the more he will fear. '. . . tribulation and anguish, on every soul of man who does evil, . . .' (Romans 2:9).

So he knows his faults, but he does not understand himself until he seeks His face and start to grow in grace. Because knowledge of the Holy One is understanding.

And then fear of Him, transformed from fear within, is the beginning of wisdom from sin.

Then torment will be sent from within, replaced be peace, joy, praise of Him and a jubilant grin having overcome sin.

But, 'He who is often rebuked, and hardens his neck, Will suddenly be destroyed, and that without remedy.' (Proverbs 29:1).

When sorting your life out, get rid of clutter, whether it is physical or mental, and keep things in one place or in as few places as possible. Don't keep moving things around. You will find things more easily then, leading to fewer frustrations. As one gets older, one becomes more forgetful. So it's best to keep things in as few places as possible.

Another Lesson

Think and speak well of others around you, and you will feel well within yourself. If you are always thinking ill and speaking ill of others while thinking well of yourself, you will nearly always look and feel miserable. This could, sooner or later, start to damage your health, not to mention your relationship with your acquaintances.

Thinking and speaking well of others or your circumstances makes you smile and brings laughter in your life. It will make you a far happier person, and your days will be much more fulfilling and full of life. This relaxes your facial muscles and probably makes you look younger and fresher too. A merry heart does good like medicine, but a broken spirit dries the bones. 94.

So make an effort not to look backwards constantly at what might have been and so *live under your past,* but instead, look forward as much as possible and *get over it.* That's what I did. Because living under your past is not life really; it is a miserable existence.

Some Conclusions

*G*iven the knowledge of how I was brought up and what I see of children today, I would not like to be a child or young person in this day and age. For example, I always had proper meals as well as three meals a day plus a lot of fun outside.

Now children are fed on fast food, becoming obese in front of a screen, with all its inherent dangers, and they are restricted from going outside through fear of others such as pedophiles. Then when they grow into young adults, they are immediately saddled with thousands of pounds of debt and little chance of getting on the housing ladder. Welcome to the age of progress.

Under the agenda of feminists and the left, girls are brought up to be more like men, taking on a lot of masculine qualities, while boys are brought up to be more like girls and more feminine, with many of their masculine attributes being condemned and dumbed down and even destroyed.

Children become parents and parents become more like children, breeding frustration on both sides in an age of correctness and sameness.

Teachers are forced to be more like pupils and be on the same level, while students become more like teachers and adults in general, often telling teachers how they should operate, even assaulting them, just as it is in the home.

The feminist movement is a well-oiled but very angry machine. And anger breeds cruelty and ultimately stupidity on a grand scale, which is what we have had for about a decade, the result of which are being felt in all quarters of society today.

Feminists and the left in general have given us a ghastly form of low-life, spiritually, financially and morally, that if they were left unchecked, they would have brought us to complete ruin.

They have brought us a loony, loutish, and ultimately lousy life, which was hardly inspiring, but which has left many trapped in obesity, poor diet, alcoholism, chain-smoking, promiscuity, family breakdown, financial breakdown, a life of lies and secrecy about things such as abortions, even multiple abortions. This has brought the country to near bankruptcy in more sense than one.

When we adopt low standards and loose principles in our lives, whether it is in the workplace, at home, or in our times of leisure, it invariably leads to disaster for ourselves and many more around us.

We would not dare allow untried, untested, and loose principles, accompanied by low standards, to build an aircraft engine, for instance, or in the way we treat the customer at work, but we allow them in our daily lives, especially in the home, without thinking about them, yet expect good results. Well, surprise, surprise, you reaped what you sowed and you got what you deserved.

Happiness in marriage depends on coming to terms with your mutual defects and dealing with them realistically. Recognise fiction; deal with facts—especially in certain vulnerable areas. Self-focus, manipulation and demanding your way can never match God's unfailing system: 'Give, and it shall be given unto you . . .' 140.

Tried and tested principles such as abstinence, chastity, respect, marriage, thrift, savings, love, entrepreneurship, hard work, and common sense have been replaced by promiscuity, shacking up, abortion, single parenthood, divorce, ASBOS, debt, hatred, benefits, and correctness. Once again, welcome to the age of progress.

As human beings, we are amazing in the many technological feats that we have achieved, but the inverse and downward spiral in our relationship with each other shows that we also have an amazing capacity for stupidity and madness on a grand scale.

Because in truth feminists have done so much damage to the family psyche and to their male counterpart under the guise of cries of distress, making it look like their man is the mess that needs redress, when in fact they are under cover dealing him something deadly to suffer as he soon discovers: 'Revenge is sweet' is the feminist cry so deadly and sly.

Yet Another Lesson

*I*n this evil age that we are living in, many women are so willing to manipulate their marriages for their own benefit and selfish ends by getting their men to fight against them and to get them to fight against each other. The end result is that politicians do not know what they are talking about when they attack fathers and husbands, as women swim in a tidal wave of anger, bitterness and deceit against what they have suffered through years of grief.

This swim is called Feminism and this anger and bitterness is to redress the balance of power so that they take over. Feminism is very unforgiving and strikes at the heart of what defines mankind to that of the feminine kind. It nearly always looks behind to drag mankind to the state of the swine.

If your wife upsets you, turn the other cheek and keep your peace. Do not react in a hasty manner, which you will almost certainly regret and others will detest, as you will have made them greatly upset. The chances are that you have enough problems of your own to deal with. Do not add to them and overburden yourself with problems you would rather not have when one ponders them over again under calmer circumstances.

Try to deal with problems you already have by chipping away at them little by little through Christ, and not adding to them. Let it all out, that which you worked so hard to hide and lay it at the feet Christ who died, but now is risen and given to you so that your sins can be forgiven. And by pondering the frequent stupidity and reckless behaviour that large sections of mankind slip so easily into, you will more easily say to yourself, 'I am not sinking to his or her level'. Then think of the countless problems you will have saved yourself then. Do not answer a fool according to his folly, lest you also be like him. 95. Wise people store up knowledge, but the mouth of the fool is near destruction. 96.

Store up knowledge, and if necessary, wait until the time is right to deal appropriately with that person. And if you wait long enough, you are more likely to show grace and forgiveness, to him or her, saving yourself and the offender a lot of grief you both probably would regret indeed.

But instead, you are now having a harvest of peace and peace of mind by allowing patience to take its full course. And as you can see, no action is needed, but for patience. And the more you practice it, the better things will get for you, leaving the other person to his or her permanent state of misery. So his or her ways don't rub off on you, just keep well away in future.

Credit Crunch and Finances

*N*ow there is a credit crunch of severe proportions, many people are taking stock of where they are and how they got there. Instead of reaping the benefits of hard work done during the long boom, they are seeing that they are losing a lot of things such as their jobs and their families, and they are more and more in debt than before. And the worse thing is that they see no way out of the hole they have got themselves into.

Even worse is the thought that if the long boom could not save us, what chance is there of this severe credit crunch turning out for the better. For many, it is proving that if they had paid more attention to their families earlier, things would not have gotten this bad.

If you are having financial difficulties in your marriage, it is easy to be tempted by offers of making money on the side or get-rich-quick ideas. Generally speaking, most of them do not work, because they all have a catch to them. And this catch benefits the proprietor and not the agent.

These schemes are not designed to make you wealthier, but quite the opposite. They are designed to get as much money out of you as possible. Once in, you may even find yourself locked into an agreement that you can't get yourself out of and you may face even worse financial ruin than when you started out.

Most of the rich have no desire to help the poor. They never had and never will. There sole aim, like vultures, is to get as much money out of you as possible, even keeping you on a string until they bleed you dry.

Many rich people think, for instance, that there are too many people on our planet today anyway, and that it would be best for most of the weak to die out, giving way to the strong. So why should they want to help you? Most of them run the system we live in by manipulation and greed, sending you the deadly seed of debt, which causes derision and division in family quarters.

If you manage to help yourself out of their trap, you might think that that's the end of that, but not so. They never leave you alone. They pester you constantly with unwanted mail of all sorts, but usually with more demands for more money. Even when you are bare, broke, ill and lonely with no one to call on, the rich will not stop hounding you for money they claim you owe them. That is the rich for you.

If you want to get wealthy, you need to chart your own course like they did. You may need help along the way, but be careful who you seek help from. Alternatively, keep looking for a job if you are willing to settle for a modest wage and a modest living. That is the best grounding to bigger things.

The choices we make in life have a profound impact for good and bad on our lifestyle and bodies. If you believe in Jesus, do not rush into hasty decisions. Be patient and watch things work out for you in the end. He will put the right people and right circumstances at the right time and place in your life, so that you don't have to regret an otherwise hasty and often reckless decision.

When couples have everything such as two cars, two or more jobs, they in fact have nothing, because they hardly see each other, let alone build their relationship. When they have less they have everything, because they see each other more and are able to build and fortify their homes and their relationships from looking elsewhere for happiness.

Break Through the Clutter and Mediocrity

So break through all the clutter, mediocrity, and dumbing down that the last decade has brought and reach for the stars in a new spirit of excellence in all areas of your life. Remember, you are all given talents from birth to make good on. The Lord expects a return on His investments.

Why settle for less when you can do your best? Shed the clutter and watch yourself rise from your solitary place of rest to be the best if you invest in progress and not allow yourself to regress to a life of painful mess.

So when you adopt *love* and *honesty* over *hate* and *dishonesty*, you experience a level of *freedom* and *victory* that is indescribable and unsurpassed by anything else, because there is no more looking over your shoulder and no more fear. There are no more burdens on your head, shoulders, or in your hearts. You also feel healthier as a result. It is a difficult, long, and hard journey indeed, once you embark on it, as you shed load after load you would rather keep. But the victory is sweeter than anything or anyone you could meet, as you gain physical and spiritual wellbeing. You may not gain immediate material wealth, but what you gain is priceless in health and wellbeing.

So in addition to helping others spiritually, this 'speculate to accumulate' is designed to help my family who has bought heavily into the promotion of secular values, man-hating tendencies, and the proliferation of single-parent values over the past thirteen years, which has cost them heavily physically, financially, and spiritually. In this evil day and age, we as Christians professing Christianity cannot afford to be messing about with the devil and his work of insanity, which brings forth nothing but vanity and futility.

Christianity in Britain, today, is critically ill to the point of death, kept alive only by a few faithful souls on fire for Christ. Christians get a fight from nearly everyone in sight. To fuel this we have a culture of soaring divorce rates, co-habitees, who are more likely to break up than married couples, single parenthood and significant proportions of children born out of wedlock. Circumstances could not be more perfect for a complete collapse in the social cohesion of this society, as policy makers show once again that they have not learnt anything from thirteen disastrous years of Labour rule, which culminated in the summer riots of 2011. And as the bible in the book of Romans says of policy makers, their foolish hearts were darkened. Professing to be wise, they became fools, . . . (Romans 1:22) So many have given up the walk and struggle, instead of becoming a crumple to those who curse and try to put you in reverse, and those who grumble.

It's only by getting up and seeing the problems and threats to our Christian lives that we can begin to grow mentally and spiritually alive, instead of the death that many want to place on our lives for fear that Christianity may survive. Likewise, it is only through painful confrontation of these problems that we learn, we win and shy away in future from making the same mistakes of sin. Anything that is not of faith is sin so don't give in.

A poem for our times.

Mankind or the Fallen Kind

We kindle the fire of hell and abandon the warmth and kindness of being brothers and just being a friend.

Embracing Babylon with both arms and abandoning the book of body, mind, heart and soul the bible.

We have fallen in love with the pennies and fallen out with people.

We love dollars and cents instead of common sense.

We have made companionship with Lucifer the loser and grieved and cut to bits all over again Christ our Lord and risen Saviour.

We prefer to wine with women and sink in sin than winning souls for the risen King.

We prefer to live a lie than a life of truth and love.

We rather be cold and calculated than offer companionship and comradeship.

We say revenge is sweet, when success can only be measured by revival and reunion when we meet.

We follow Satan and sink in sin rather than try to follow the Son most times and bring out the sunshine of our King.

We hate, dishonour and so disobey the Son, rather than love, honour and obey because His time is soon to come.

We rather die holding on to secrets and sin than live by letting go of all that's within.

The initial pain of letting go of your burden of sin and your filthy bin is far outweighed by a life of love, lift, lessons learnt and a jubilant grin.

Winning using the underhand thing is preferred to wisdom and understanding.

Standing tall and making someone feel small is preferred to answering the call of someone trapped by life's painful fall.

Wisdom and understanding now take a back seat to the underhand thing.

Being truthful and trustworthy are now true casualties of immorality.

Imitating iniquity is now commonplace for grudge, greed and dishonest deeds.

When injustice becomes the law of the land it's up to the upright and just to resist till we regain the upper hand.

When life has become a facade of lie and deceit, we pay the price through rebellion, bankruptcy and defeat.

It's now every man for himself or every self to destroy his fellow man.

It's win by any means as long as your fellow man does not know that you have set him up for a dreadful blow.

What a sad and sordid state as the fallen kind becomes so irate, that he lends a listening ear to Satan's bate and falls to his silent but rotting state.

Give the boot to Satan and sin; obey Christ and His divine thing, so that He gives you a new life and confines your old life to the waste bin.

Now confess your sin of that dreadful and ugly thing that's making your heart, mind and soul a frightful looking and filthy waste bin.

Stop making them too numerous, too filthy for even you yourself to stomach the stench of setting the record straight to family and friends, some of whom may have already caught wind of the fact that you are having enough of this erroneous and dreadful thing.

This Once Great Place

We substitute Christ the risen King for Satan and sin and worship the creation instead of the creator and made a blooming mess of mankind's address. What a terrifying state this once terrific and great place has become because of greed, selfishness and trying to prevent the loss of face.

Well, will we ever learn that our time and place in this still great place is not to serve oneself only, lest we all fall on our face, but to serve and help save every good, bad and ugly face of this God's great human race.

Then pay respect, honour and homage to our Lord and Saviour who paid that awful price to cover all our disgrace. So that God could find us acceptable in his home, heaven, a great and everlasting place.

What a great and wonderful day that will be when God's place for the human race will finally be found and happily given to those who were willing to pay the price of self-sacrifice.

But likewise, what an awful and dreadful day for the self-serving soul, who has made his way and payday at the expense of the unsuspecting, the simple and the servitude soul.

How can you too expect the best when you have dealt again the hand of death to the Lord Jesus Christ and to all His just and faithful followers whom you never gave any rest from this world's mess.

If you mess with evil you will level with the devil. And that's an awful place because it will only end in disgrace. Take heed and be strong indeed that you don't fall prey to the man or woman of greed.

Because while you wallow in pity to have fallen to the man of the City, the man of greed will have done well indeed until his day to fall prey to the God of the day, the God of might and the God of right.

And what a terrible and awful sight from the blight of heart, soul and sight when the Lord ignites that bright but terrible light, yet dark and obscure from the Lord's righteous and long-suffering souls who have been given heaven's cure from those now covered in sores.

Be diligent, be sure that you've found the long, righteous path and cure that leads to life that endure and not the quick path of ease that leads ultimately to death and disease; or the way in which many have become prey to this the devil's way.

Labour became the party of bankers and benefit scroungers that pocket the money of hard working mothers and fathers who live hand to mouth instead, while the parasites take the largest bite nations bread, leaving the hard working majority with no authority over the nation's money.

What a travesty of justice when some can live easy lives and buy nice houses from benefits and double-dealing tactics, yet never pay any taxes. Then the burden to support such a system falls on the fuming middle majority who is sinking under the weight of his tax take being sneaked to the promotion of single parenthood at the expense of the common good.

No wonder the mess that we are in is caused by that parasitic few, that poke fun and grin at the system we live in whereby the majority try hard to do the right thing, but with no reward coming in.

Worklessness and worthlessness has become the highway and byway to rights and gifts of benefits and credits, while the overworked and under-paid have become the drainpipe for this class and type to get their way everyday.

It is great to be saved by grace and faith and not held bondage by the disgrace that fate placed on us by some of our loved ones whose sole interest is self-interest as long we succumb to what they would have us become.

What a cruel twist of fate from those God saved by His goodness and grace to those that would have us become a useless and worthless mess of their likeness.

The power of grace and faith is my embrace to fling my failings and man's debating of my lack of success, not knowing that I am yet to see God's best and put to rest the awful mess I hitherto made of the Lord's niceness.

What a frightful and dreadful way Lucifer has made many of God's fragile and precious little things not fit for His heavenly thing. What a frightful and dreadful way Lucifer has made most of God's precious and fragile little things refuse to be fit for His soon and coming King, but fit instead to fling in hell's fiery bin.

The foolishness of God has hardened the heart of the fool with his money; making the taste of honey so sweet he does not even know that he has both feet firmly fitted in filth, misery and fire indeed.

God gave us the good, the bad and the ugly to give us a sense of right, wrong and the downright funny. So go forth and make honey and money, but remember God is the author and finisher of your destiny, whether it is heaven solely or hell only. So do good and bring glad tidings to the poor and needy, and the Lord will reward you with the same measure and more in heaven and eternity.

Can't you see oh man, oh fool, that this world is no longer cool. It is becoming a dreadful thing with poverty, crimes of depravity, wars, famine, earthquakes, volcanoes, bankruptcies and of course the certainty of the second coming of our wonderful Lord and Saviour Jesus Christ the eternal and risen King.

In a dream a few years ago he told me a thing, "Make your mind up whether you are going to serve Me or not, so that I can prepare for the second coming," of our Lord and risen King. So by boiling the midnight oil and writing this book, I have done part of His divine thing. He was making plain to me that things were coming to the boil whereby we will all be rewarded for our toil.

For the many it will be a weeping and a waling. For it is time for the eternal union with the enemy of their making. While for the few who toiled, laboured and suffered for so long at their wicked hands, it will be joy and peace at long last that we have finally been freed from our bondage of poverty, depravity and persecution of which there will be no further repetition, but by joining instead the overwhelming joy of the new and everlasting resurrection.

So He says come my child, there is no time to be shy. Stop messing with the filth and the fly by joining the Lords chosen few and not become one of hell's stew. Because it will soon be time to bid farewell and goodbye to this wayward world and join Him in a most beautiful place where time and lack of space is not of mine, but dwell in safety from hell, where all will be safe, full of grace, easy paced and well.

To our Lord a day is like a thousand years and a thousand years like a day. So don't dismay at their evil way, because God don't do things in a hurry, nor does He delay. He takes His time to get all things right. So you too be patient and not hurry. For to those who hurry, there is a pit and they won't spot it until they lie face down at the bottom of it to fit.

The battle at the end will be the greatest to defend. But stay the course of life, because near the finishing line don't be blind to the wiles of mankind. And if we are bold and not go cold, the prize for finishing in front will be an affront to their evil and wicked stunt.

Men will be vile and revile your very existence, because of your persistence in pressing for the Gospel and its expansion into cities and the outer regions.

What a beautiful day that will be when we can say 'thank God for being true to His word, to me and to those who helped to save me.'

So long my child, but don't be bold yet blind. It is better to be shy and not cry, than to be bitter then having to be twice shy.

Then the words of God I read before nearly completing this book based on the daily prayer reading booklet, *The Word for Today* are the words by Hosea 10:12, 'Sow for yourselves righteousness; reap in mercy; break up the fallow ground, for it is time to seek the Lord, till he comes and rains righteousness on you.'

Messages from Our Lord

from disc called Audio Extracts Journal of the 'Unknown Prophet':

Therefore to the independent soul the Lord gave me the following message—

Track 5: TO THOSE EXPERIENCING WEARINESS

"Dearly beloved, I know you are weary. I see you so worn down by the cares and pressures of each day, that you have almost lost sight of My hand upon your life. Oh beloved, as you enter the end of the age, so shall the pressures increase. So shall your need for times of refreshing become more desperate.

For you see without Me you are nothing. Apart from Me you are able to do nothing. In your own strength, in your own power, you will be continually frustrated and unable to accomplish all you have need of.

For it is only in a vital, continual union with Me as the source of your life, that you shall be, in these end-times, able to survive. And so I have drawn you to a place where I will be your very breath—where communion with Me will be your very reason for existence each day—where nothing less will sustain you.

I've drawn you to a deeper place in the spirit, where your need for My presence will be so consuming, that unless you draw close to Me, the

CARES and the STRESSES of LIFE, even of MY CALL UPON YOU will OVER-WELM YOU.

For you see beloved, I call you to abide in Me. The FATHER and I seek for these times with whom We can make Our abode. We seek worshipers in spirit and in truth. We seek those who hunger for Our fellowship. We seek those who thirst for Our presence. And through these ones, through this communion, so shall Our presence overflow through My Body in the great works prophesied.

So shall our lives manifest in greater miracles, in greater healings, in greater exploits, in greater evangelism, in greater conviction of sin that has yet ever been released upon the earth.

So come, come My child, come, come My minister—you who are weary—come to Me. For I am your rest; I am your refreshing; I am your anointing; I AM YOUR ALL."

Track 13: SEDUCTION, LUST AND JEZEBEL

"This assignment in more easily discerned, but far more lethal in it's outward consequences. For it devours its prey. The intense seduction lures My children into the enticement of sin, but eventually leaves them stripped of their ministry, calling, reputation and sometimes even their relationship with Myself and the Father and their eternal salvation." He sighed deeply.

The Father knows that these very ones who were drawn to Him because they knew the very weakness of their own souls. Like the woman whose story I promised would be told eternally."

I (prophet) spoke, 'The woman who washed her feet? Jesus smiled tenderly.

"Those who have been forgiven much love much. In this last generation many came to us from the greatest ensnarements and bondages. Once they saw Our great love for them, they became our greatest champions and bondservants.

For their gratitude for receiving such a redemption was unfathomable. These are the ones who would come close and tender with Me and which follow me unto death."

'But if they would follow you unto death, Lord Jesus, and they hear your voice, then how would they fall to seducing spirits?' I (prophet) asked. That chill gripping me again and sensing the answer.

"Every weakness that these ones experienced in their lives," His expression was so grave, "Every fisher, each wound, each broken place that lies unhealed, these satanic powers and principalities and demons shall now target."

"Many, many of my children did not receive healing of their minds, emotions and souls in this last generation. And because they have lived in the household of God for years, many do not even realise that these scarred places exist.

These last days' assignments have been meticulously strategised and that is the very strength of their evil.

They have been taylor-made to each of My champions. They know the urgent, driving, unmet needs of the soul. the generational bondages of each individual CALLED BY ME TO IMPACT THIS GENERATION; the lack of nurturing; the deep unhealed rejections and hurts of the emotion; the fatherlessness, the need for affirmation, the desire to belong; the deep isolation—all of which were not met in Me, now lay the perfect snare for the assignments of the enemy.

My champions shall now know a violent satanic assailing against their minds. Any thought not taken captive, shall be a thought that can take violent root in their souls to lead to ensnarement. Anything from their past that has been dealt with by their own strength and not by My spirit, shall become a snare to them and shall leave them vulnerable to the enemy of their souls. Any habit not ruthlessly dealt with and put to the cross, when assigned with the searing heat of temptation will bread and rapidly multiply," Jesus continued.

"In this past age Jezebel has translated itself in many different forms. But one of her primary rules in this age is her amalgamation with Babylon: the spirit of the world and lust; lust of the flesh; lust of the eyes and the pride of life. Jezebel rules electronic media: film, television and advertising. She is the epitome of seduction in this last age. She was Delilah, Salomé, Herodotus. She rules pornography, adultery, lasciviousness, homosexuality, pride, power, separation, divorce, and ambition and every sin and perversion of the flesh known to mankind. She tantalises, packages sin, sells it, and these bases exposes their victim before killing.

Her primary targets in this last church age are My ministers—both men and women."

'I felt the icy chill once more.'

"Well I know the depth of hatred Jezebel holds for God's bondservants. Multitudes of My ministers today struggle with pornography. Multitudes of My ministers struggle with lust on a daily basis.

Multitudes are struggling with a terrible *coldness of heart within their marriages* and families. Many came out of deeply sinful lifestyles or out of deep-rooted rejections. And as was the way in this past generation, many of My children were not discipled effectively and did not receive effective healing in the areas that propelled them in that habitual sin.

Also, especially among My leaders in this past generation, My church has been embroiled in self righteousness. And if one of My children has cried for help in an area of failure, many times they have been ostracised, isolated and have their confidence betrayed. This has led to My ministers leading double lives. Having a public face for their congregations, while crying out to Me in their bed-chambers, because they hate what they have become. But they know many will deal treacherously with them if they admit their need for help.

Jezebel knows this full well, and it is one of her most effective strategies. For once the champion has been isolated from real help, the seducing spirits are unleashed and time after time my child falls into adultery, fornication, homosexuality, pornography, separation and divorce.

And how My Father and I grieve, for well Lucifer knows that it was often for those who love Us and who have hungered for Our presence, who have often been the most damaged in their past. And now Satan targets the damaged places.

WARN THEM, WARN THEM TO GUARD AGAINST THE GREAT DECEIVER OF THEIR SOULS. For like Satan came to Me in the wilderness, he intends to do now to those who follow Me, who lead others, to tempt, to lure. For in this most violent of testings, even My most elect shall fall."

'He hesitated and a great pain seem to cloud His countenance. And I sensed that He was thinking about one I knew that He loved greatly, that had been caught that month in a prevailing sin, and I thought of ones this past year who have fallen in ways that have been politically acceptable to us in the household of God.

But my thoughts were not with those, but rather with those—so many of late—that have fallen morally. Not acceptable. And who have lost and taken time out of their ministries. And as I looked into Jesus's eyes, I knew that these were the ones that He grieved for. For well He knew how they loved Him. In fact some loved Him more, more than any others.

And how well He knew how they must have wrestled in the still quiet hours of the early morning against sin. But because the assignments of hell have been so meticulously crafted and because Lucifer knew so well that the politics of the church so often ensured isolation and silence in struggling with sin, one by one they had fallen to the brokeness and fishers in their own souls.

And has He looked at me I felt suddenly how He looked upon that rich young man. And so I prayed for ALL of us that had been targeted by the enemy to be assailed in this last end time. That even in the tumult and the fierce heat of the testings and trials and temptations we would draw on His strength that would take us through the eye of the needle, to that last lap of the narrow way that we may be counted as conquerers.

Lord Jesus how can we stand?' I whispered.

"There is only one way to survive the onslaught my child," His voice was so soft. "Firstly, to repent of any and of all luke warmness and backsliding in your heart, and to reignite and maintain zealously your first love for Me. Secondly, to keep yourself from all idols and remain fervent in the Spirit, which is the result of true fellowship in Spirit and in truth with MYSELF and with the FATHER. And on feeding on my word until my word is spirit and life to you."

He hesitated and finally the cross. "The deception in every temptation is that which caused Adam to lead billions of souls into sin; that of selfishness; temptation promises that which self desires. When My children desires the promises of sin more that they desire Me, they will fall.

The greatest weapon to survive the onslaught is for My children to take up their cross and to follow me. To take up the cross daily and to die to everything in their souls and their minds which opposes My truth; To let go of that lower life which is the flesh, and continually mortify their minds and their bodies, and to put to death the deeds of the flesh.

My children have forgotten the power of the cross. They have thought that to die once is sufficient. But the spirit of the world with its carnality and selfishness loosed upon this present generation is so strong in these evil days, that it is only in a continual daily crucifying of their flesh that they will indeed be able to withstand temptation.

Remember it is written, "For we do not have a High Priest who is unable to understand and sympathise and have a shared feeling with our weaknesses and infirmities and liabilities to the assault of temptation. But One who has been tempted in every respect as we are yet without sinning."

Even when you are feeling that you are falling in the very pit of hell itself; Even when it seems you are clinging to Me and My Father and to My word and its principles by a thread; When you feel that hell is sucking you in; It is then that you must cry out to Me, cry out to My Father, cry out our name. And in that very second We will come to you and rescue you. We will draw you in and protect you from every wile of the evil one.

I said that I will never forsake you and this is true. Even when you are in the heat of temptation; Still if you cry out to Me, I will hear you.

SPEAK MY WORD AND I THE LIVING WORD WILL COME TO YOUR AID, and accomplish that which I have promised.

Now warn My children, My father's heart is grieved with a terrible grieving. Warn My beloved that many will be saved out of the fowler's snare. That even those in the deepest mire might cry out to Me and FIND THEIR WAY HOME.

The Coming Day of the Lord

. . . knowing this first: that scoffers will come in the last days, walking according to their own lusts and saying, "Where is the promise of His coming? . . ." 97.

But the heavens and the earth, which are now preserved by the same word, are reserved for fire until the day of judgement and perdition of ungodly men. 98.

The Lord is not slack concerning His promise, as some count slackness, but is long-suffering toward us, not willing that any should perish, but that all should come to repentance. 99.

But the day of the Lord will come as a thief in the night, in which the heavens will pass away with a great noise, and the elements will melt with fervent heat; both the earth and the works that are in it will be burned up. 100.

Nevertheless we, according to His promise, look for new heavens and a new earth in which righteousness dwells. 101.

Therefore beloved, looking forward to these things, be diligent to be found by Him in peace, without spot and blameless; . . . 102.

Satan is allowed to buffet us to rest in his sunset and become a loser to our accuser and a son and daughter of the midnight hour or to get the picture to resist the ultimate loser and be raptured as pure for heaven's cure.

But that would require us overcoming at least some of our demons to become Christ's real ones, achieve our potential in the material, spiritual, and physical dimensions.

So when He asks us what did we do with our talent, we can say, 'we did not relent until we became Your heaven sent'.

We are only dust hence possess an inherent weakness to slide into Satan's sickness, sleepiness and backwardness. But after feeling his every pain do we still suffer and become insane, sliding further into hell's domain, bringing more and more pain?

Or do we make plain that its time to make gain and possible fame from being buffeted into the drain, but now to become the best we were meant to be in this life and the life to be, despite all around being death, regress and madness.

The roads to life and death are like our motorways and byways. The motorways are wide and fast, where many can relax at last, and it is the path the majority use to get away from the city blues. Some are so comfortable, that they fall asleep at the wheels. While the rich in their huge expensive vehicles are usually in the fast lane, having no shame of driving beyond the pale at speeds that are insane . . . for wide is the gate and broad is the way that leads to destruction, and there are many who go in by it. 1. And it is easier for the camel to enter through the eye of a needle, than for the rich man to enter into the Kingdom of Heaven.

The A roads and B roads are far more narrow and difficult to negotiate by comparison, needing both hands on the wheels to keep on your side of the road and away from the hedgerows. In addition, you have to go slowly because of the difficulty in getting by. So . . . narrow is the gate and difficult is the way which leads to life, and there are few who find it. 1.

The riots in our cities are a sure sign that there is something significant missing in our families, which is a breakdown in morality and our broken families. So we sow the wind and reap the whirlwind. 103. Yes, we sow in sin and now have the regurgitated thing, with News International also becoming news international.

Wake up to the choices we face, yes this great human race and take your place out of disgrace and that messy place and into Christ's saving grace.

The Choice is yours!!!

God uses unlikely vessels for His collosal tasks such as Jeremiah, who suffered from grave depression and said such things as 'cursed be the day that I was born.' Nonetheless, he achieved what he was given to do.

The Lord has also chosen me, Philip Michael Mattis, another unlikely vessel, who has suffered decades of grave depressions, who has been used and abused, hated and berated, spat on and sat upon, riled and reviled by men and children to do another of his collosal tasks in these the end times. Philip meaning lover of horses and one of Christ's first disciples; Michael meaning God-like or next to God; and Mattis a match to set the sleepy on light, He has sent to warn His people using the book of Jeremiah again.

Because He said to me, I warned them in the days of Noah, I warned them at Babel, at Sodom and again today, but my people have turned away from Me. So He has sent me from that grave City to a rural enclave. For the fate of that City is no debate when Christ finally closes the gates. So when the Stock Markets of the great cities of the East and the West finally collapse, and those who rule the world by manipulation and greed, at the expense of those in need, see their idols for what they truly are, then they will know that the end is near.

He said, "Before I formed you in the womb I knew you; Before you were born I sanctified you; I ordained you a prophet to the nations." 104.

"Do not be afraid of their faces, For I am with you to deliver you," says the Lord. 105.

". . . My people have changed their Glory for what does not profit. Be astonished, O heavens, at this, And be horribly afraid; Be very desolate," says the Lord.

"For my people have committed two evils; They have forsaken Me, the fountain of living waters, and hewn themselves cisterns—broken cisterns that can hold no water." 106. Broken cisterns of the world such as stocks and shares, gold, silver and armaments.

"Blow the trumpet in the land; Cry; 'Gather together.' And say, 'Assemble yourselves, and let us go into the fortified cities.' Set up the standard toward Zion. Take refuge! Do not delay! For I will bring disaster from the north and great destruction."

The lion has come up from his thicket, and the destroyer of nations is on his way. He has gone forth from his place to make your land desolate. Your cities will be laid waste without inhabitant. For this, clothe yourself with sackcloth, lament and wail. For the **fierce anger** of the Lord has not turned back from us. 107.

"Most assuredly, I say to you, he who believes in Me, the works that I do, he will do also; and greater works than these he will do, because I go to my Father." 108.

For we do not have a High Priest who cannot sympathise with our weaknesses, but was in all points tempted as we are, yet without sin.

Let us therefore come boldly to the throne of grace, that we may obtain mercy and find grace to help in time of need. 109.

I waited patiently for the Lord;

And He inclined to me,

And heard my cry.

He also brought me up out of a horrible pit.

Out of the miry clay,

And set my feet upon a rock,

And established my steps.

He has put a new song in my mouth-

Praise to our God;

Many will see it and fear,

And will trust in the Lord. 133.

... being confident of this very thing, that He who has begun a good work in you will complete it until the day of Jesus Christ; 134.

Philip Mattis

Notes

1. Matthew 7:13, 14
2. Proverbs 9:10
3. Proverbs 18:2
4. Romans 12:10-12
5. Romans 12:14
6. Romans 12:17, 18
7. Romans 12:21
8. Isaiah 54:17
9. Luke 17:3
10. Mark 10:29-31
11. Philippians 2:3
12. Matthew 5:22
13. Ephesians 4:31
14. Matthew 19:6
15. Ephesians 5:22, 23
16. Proverbs 19:11
17. Proverbs 13:10
18. Proverbs 17:14
19. Ephesians 5:15
20. Proverbs 13:3
21. Proverbs 15:1, 2
22. Proverbs 14:1
23. Proverbs 14:3
24. James 1:2-4
25. James 1:12, 19
26. James 3:5-8
27. James 3:17, 18
28. 2 Timothy 3:1-4
29. 2 Timothy 3:1-4
30. Titus 2:1-7
31. Titus 3:1-3
32. Ephesians 6:1-4
33. Ephesians 4:2, 3
34. Ephesians 4:14, 15
35. Ephesians 4:29
36. Ephesians 5:3, 4
37. Ephesians 5:28, 29
38. Proverbs 13:13-16
39. Proverbs 24:21, 22
40. Ephesians 5:11-13
41. Proverbs 16:5
42. Proverbs 18:12

43. Proverbs 13:20
44. Proverbs 24:25
45. Titus 2:3-7
46. Romans 3:13-18
47. Proverbs 31:3
48. Matthew 10:21, 36
49. Proverbs 9:10
50. Proverbs 18:2
51. Proverbs 16:18
52. Proverbs 15:1
53. Proverbs 16:32
54. Matthew 7:13, 14
55. Proverbs 10:14
56. Proverbs 13:3
57. Proverbs 12:15
58. Proverbs 12:18
59. Proverbs 15:4
60. Proverbs. 18:2
61. James 5:16
62. Proverbs 14:32
63. Proverbs 13:21
64. Proverbs 13:15
65. Proverbs 11:17
66. Proverbs 11:3
67. Proverbs 4:19
68. Proverbs 16:18
69. Proverbs 19:9
70. Proverbs 13:3
71. Matthew 11:28, 30
72. Proverbs 13:14
73. Proverbs 13:15
74. Proverbs 11:9
75. Genesis 2:18
76. Genesis 2:24
77. Proverbs 29:15
78. Proverbs 29:17
79. Proverbs 13:16
80. Proverbs 19:11
81. Proverbs 25:26
82. Proverbs 26:12
83. Proverbs 14:17
84. Proverbs 14:15
85. Proverbs 14:29
86. Proverbs 16:18
87. Proverbs 16:16
88. Proverbs 16:7
89. Proverbs 9:10
90. 1 Corinthians 3:18
91. 2 Corinthians 2:11
92. Proverbs 15:22
93. Proverbs 24:6
94. Proverbs 17:23
95. Proverbs 26:4
96. Proverbs 10:14
97. **2 Peter 3:3, 4**
98. **2 Peter 3:7**
99. **2 Peter 3:9**
100. **2 Peter 3:10**
101. **2 Peter 3:13**
102. **2 Peter 3:14**

103. **Hosea 8:7**
104. Jeremiah 1:5
105. Jeremiah 1:8
106. Jeremiah 2:11-13
107. Jeremiah 4:5-8
108. John 14:12
109. Hebrews 4:15, 16
110. Proverbs 25:26
111. Philippians 4:13
112. Matthew 8:23
113. 1 Samuel 3:13 (NIV)
114. James 1:19
115. Ecclesiastes 5:2, 3
116. Galations 5:22-23
117. Romans 6:12-16 (NLT)
118. Proverbs 16: (NLT)
119. Matthew 16:24 (NIV)
120. Matthew 10:39
121. Genesis 39:9 (NIV)
122. 1 Corinthians 10:12 (NCV)
123. James 1:13-15 (TM)
124. James 1:12 (NIV)
125. Luke 15:11-16 (NIV)
126. Luke 15:24 (NIV)
127. Proverbs 27:22
128. Proverbs 18:15
129. 2 Timothy 4:13
130. John 14:6
131. 2 Corinthians 4:2 (TM)
132. 2 Corinthians 1:13 (TM)

133. Psalm 40:1-3
134. Philippians 1:6
135. Matthew 10:35, 36
136. Ecclesiastes 1:8 (NAS)
137. Hebrew 13:5 (KJV)
138. Philippians 4:11 (KJV)
139. Ecclesiastes 9:9 TM
140. Luke 6:38 (KJV)
141. Proverbs 16:7
142. Proverbs 122:6 (NLT)
143. Luke 3:4-6
144. Colossians 3:12-14
145. 2 Timothy 4:7, 8
146. 2 Corinthians 4:9 (TLB)
147. Philippians 4:13 (TLB)
148. 2 Corinthians 4:8-9 (TLB)

Portrait Drawings

As part of my book I have included four of my drawings, one of an unknown female, one of Colin Powell, former American Secretary of State and former American Presidents Jimmy Carter and Ronald Reagan in a spirit of excellence, thus ditching the Labour years of dumbing down and mediocrity and reaching for the stars, which we should all be aiming for.

With this photograph which the Lord has taken on my camera, whereby he has supernaturally superimposed a clock face on the sun on 7 different photographs, he has asked me to tell the world that time is short and that He is, "The voice of one crying in the wilderness: 'Prepare the way of the Lord; make His paths straight. Every valley shall be filled and every mountain and hill brought low; The crooked places shall be made straight and the rough ways smooth; And all flesh shall see the salvation of God.'" 143.

Then the last words He left with me for completing this book are, 'Therefore, as the elect of God, holy and beloved, put on tender mercies, kindness, humility, meekness, longsuffering; bearing with one another, and forgiving one another, if anyone has a complaint against another; even has Christ forgave you, so you also must do. But above all these things put on love, which is the bond of perfection. 144.

I have fought the good fight, I have finished the race, I have kept the faith. Finally, there is laid up for me the crown of righteousness, which the Lord, the righteous judge, will give to me on that Day, and not to me only but also to all who have loved His appearing. 145.

Ways in which the Lord has helped me directly with this book: After scrolling to my desired page on my computer, the Lord would scroll back automatically to the page that He thinks I should be paying attention to in order to make corrections. Then I saw clearly what needed correcting. He did this about ten times in total. In addition, after making my corrections, he moved the curser automatically to the next correction that needed to be made on the same page. He did this once. All I had to do was sit back and marvel at the curser and the scroll bar moving in a manner that appeared to be on their own.

Finally, the insertions from UCB's The Word for Today, were placed in front of me, without me have to search or research. And He pointed out exactly where He wanted those insertions to go, by giving me the Spirit to know just how He intends to run this show.

References from:

Unicef Report 2007
Disc called Audio Extracts Journal of the 'Unknown Prophet'
The Proper Care and Feeding of Marriage by Dr Laura Schlessinger
UCB's The Word for Today by Bob and Debby Gass with Ruth Gass Halliday.
All scripture references are from the New King James Version, and the King
    James Version, unless otherwise noted.
AMP Amplified Bible
NIV New International Version
NAS new American Standard
TM The Message
NRS New Revised Standard Version

PHPS Philips N. T. in Modern English
GWT God's World Translation
TEV Today's English Version
NEB New English Bible

How to contact UCB:

General Enquires
UCB Operations Centre,
Westport Road
Stoke-on-Trent, ST6 4JF
T 0845 60 40 401 (local rate call)
E ucb@ ucb.co.uk
W ucb.co.uk
UCB Broadcasting Enquiries

T 01782 642 000
W ucbmedia.co.uk
E info@ucbmedia.co.uk

UCB Northern Ireland
Commission Broadcast Centre
Ballyoran Lane
BELFAST
BT16 1XJ
T 028 9028 2000

Free issues of the daily devotional Word for Today are available for the UK
and Republic of Ireland.

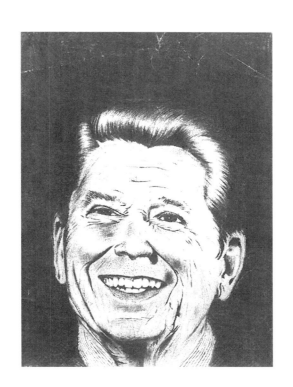

Phil visiting UCB radio studios.

What a beautiful day when this book reaches the hearts
of they that choose to forsake the wayward way.

The awesome beauty of nature and our loving creator.

That sun is no fun.

The beauty of the flower leaves one in awe and wonder.

The sun and the clock at 8:45: the time the Lord told me
to send my finished manuscript to my publishers.

The prayer garden at UCB studios.

Another sun and clock at 9'oclock, so isn't it time to take stock?

Perplexing cloud formation over our nation.

The darkness and the light, Oh what a sight.

Can one see the images above, or is one too stuck to fly like a dove?

That gloom shall be removed for the dawn of light into God's insight.

Phil with the car he uses for his driving lessons.

The sun and the cloud looking so beautiful and proud.

The beautiful British countryside is a place to hide.

Lightning Source UK Ltd.
Milton Keynes UK
UKOW050141030212

186547UK00002B/13/P